THE

COURT OF THE TUILERIES

Vol. I.

The Court of the Tuileries, *FROM THE RESTORATION TO THE FLIGHT OF LOUIS PHILIPPE. BY CATHERINE CHARLOTTE, LADY JACKSON*

IN TWO VOLUMES
VOLUME I.

WILDSIDE PRESS

Large Paper Edition

This edition is limited to one
thousand copies, of which
this is Number....139.

CONTENTS OF VOL. I.

CONTENTS vii

LIST OF ILLUSTRATIONS

VOLUME I.

COURT OF THE TUILERIES

————◆————

CHAPTER I.

INTRODUCTORY.

"YOU may do everything, and you dare nothing. For once, then, be daring."

Thus wrote the arch-intriguer Prince Talleyrand to the allied sovereigns and their generals; and to those words and the effect they produced, far more than to the plotting, intriguing, and treachery going on on all sides in Paris, the Bourbons may be said mainly to have owed their restoration to the throne of France. For on the 23d of March, 1814, Napoleon, having reached St. Dizier, put to the rout a corps of Russian cavalry, whose movements were intended to mislead him as to the actual direction in which the main body of the allied army was marching. Aware, however, that the Austrians and Prussians were marching on Paris, he determined on an audacious and desperate plan for checking their advance, and gaining time, as he hoped, to reach the capital before them — the route of Troyes being then open to him.

The Director of the Posts, Général de La Valette, had recently despatched a warning message to Napoleon. "The partisans of the foreigner," he wrote, "are holding up their heads, and are seconded by secret intrigues. The presence of the emperor is needed, and there is not a moment to lose if the capital is to be saved."

Immediately Général Dejean is sent forward to announce the emperor's speedy arrival, and to bear his orders to the lieutenant-general, Joseph Bonaparte, and the minister of war, the Duc de Feltre, to resist to the last extremity; to barricade the streets; to fortify the houses; to cut the outer bridges and take away the boats; to bring eighty field-pieces of large calibre from Cherbourg and place them in battery; to surround Paris' with redoubts, and hold out till he came. To this he added, — unfortunately, as the disastrous results proved, — "If the enemy should advance on the capital with a force so overwhelming that to resist it would be impossible, send away the empress-regent and my son, with the officers of the household and the ministers, in the direction of the Loire, for I am about to manœuvre in a manner that will probably leave you some days without any news of me."

The emperor's manœuvres were indeed so mysterious — announcing some new and striking proof of his genius and great fertility in expedients — that they considerably disquieted the allies, and caused them great embarrassment. The Emperor Alexander especially regarded their harassing consequences with alarm — so much so, that the question whether it would not be prudent to avoid incurring the risk of being shut up between insurgent provinces, Napoleon's army, — weakened though it was, — and a city that could furnish 100,000 combatants, was actually under deliberation when M. de Talleyrand's missive reached headquarters.

By the same messenger the royalist committee in Paris vaunted their successes in the South. Hesitation was at once banished from the council of the allies. The interrupted march on the capital was speedily resumed, and the army, divided into three columns, pressed onward by forced marches, eager to reach the city, whose inhabitants — as M. de Talleyrand would fain have them believe, and as the Duc d'Alberg also sent them word — were anxiously waiting to welcome them with palms of victory, and laurel wreaths for the conquerors' brows.

In the night of the 29th, Napoleon with his guard had pushed forward fifteen leagues. But in his impatience to reach Paris ere it was too late, he determined to precede his troops — disregarding the risk he thus ran of falling into the hands of the enemy. In a *calèche* with post-horses, and accompanied by Généraux Berthier and Caulaincourt, he dashes on with great speed, and at ten in the evening of the 30th halts at Fromenteau. He is then but five leagues from his capital. But there he encounters Général Belliard marching with a small force towards Fontainebleau. With dejected air the general reveals the fatal intelligence — Paris had capitulated only two hours before. The empress-regent, whose escort had withdrawn from the defence of the city 2,500 troops, the lieutenant-general, the ministers, etc., had all left for Blois, with the exception of M. de Talleyrand — *forcibly* detained in Paris to welcome the enemy, and to play the part of King of France *ad interregnum*.

Under this desperate blow of adverse fate Napoleon is for a moment bewildered. He alights from his carriage, and, reclining on the stone seat of a fountain, becomes wrapped in thought. Speedily, however, he recovers his wonted *sang-froid;* directs the Duc de Vicenza, M. de Caulaincourt, to repair to Paris, to obtain his intervention in the treaty ; then orders his horses' heads to be turned towards Fontainebleau.

Already he meditates a new campaign.

"Two hours ago," he murmured, as the carriage drove off ; and truly they were words that must have given rise to very bitter reflections.

Two hours later — had not capitulation been pressed upon Joseph Bonaparte by Maréchaux Marmont and Mortier, with undue haste — and the emperor had been in Paris, when, in the words of one who accompanied the allied armies, "a very different scene would have been enacted from that which actually took place." The capitulation was signed at the headquarters of the allied sovereigns at two in the morning of the 31st of March. At seven, the troops of Maréchaux Marmont and Mortier were to evacuate the city, and at noon the conquering heroes to make their triumphal entry into it.

CHAPTER II.

A Band of Traitors. — A Mysterious Agency. — The Traitor
Marmont. — A Polite Attention. — " Where Is He ? Where
Is He ? " — Entry of the Allied Armies. — A Well-deserved
Soufflet. — The Emblem of Victory. — *Belles Amies de M. de
Talleyrand.* — The White Cockades. — Alexander and Fred-
erick William. — " *Vive Henri Quatre !* "

HE shoutings, acclamations, and vociferous *vivas* that greeted the foreign
sovereigns and their troops on their
entry into the capital of France would have eter-
nally disgraced the nation had they been a spon-
taneous outburst of welcome on the part of the
people. The allies themselves were amazed, as
well they might be, at the uproarious enthusiasm
with which conquered Paris seemed to glory over
its own humiliation. The page of history has
not recorded many such scenes ; for probably no
other beleaguered city ever contained within its
walls such a band of traitors — both men and
women — so eagerly bent on delivering it into the
hands of a hostile force, for the furtherance of
their own petty personal interests.

The allies were indebted for the ovation that
greeted them to the active exertions of M. de
Talleyrand, and the self-styled royalist committee,

of which he was the head, the soul, and the guiding spirit. Otherwise the boulevards would have been silent and deserted. As it was, the *bourgeoisie*, and all in whose breasts there glowed a spark of patriotism, remained in their houses. Most persons, too, who had anything to lose, were anxious and disquieted concerning their property — naturally regarding with dread the influx of rough soldiers, who were shortly to be quartered upon them, and let loose on the city to indulge with little or no restraint their destructive and pillaging propensities.

The municipality of Paris seemed to have abdicated. The police were nowhere to be seen. A few wounded soldiers, who were being conveyed to the hospitals, and here and there a straggler or deserter, alone represented the French army. Nothing had been done for the defence of Paris. Some mysterious agency seemed to favour the invaders, and to thwart and paralyse every effort to obstruct or delay their triumph. Suspicion pointed towards the minister of war, — the Duc de Feltre, — believed to be acting in concert with Talleyrand.

Very little fighting preceded the capitulation. The students of the military colleges and some of the old *Invalides* behaved gallantly at the barrier of Clichy, under the veteran Général Moncey. Of course their spirited resistance, unsupported, was soon overcome, and these posts, by arrangement, were then occupied by the national guards. They, however, were not trusted with arms, lest indignation should rouse them to attempt the repulse of the enemy; while Maréchaux Marmont and Mortier waited not for the morning dawn to evacuate the city, but passed out of it in the night.

Marmont on the following day gave over to Général Souham the command of his corps of 15,000 men — first, for the greater convenience of carrying on a secret negotiation with M. de Talleyrand and Prince Schwarzenberg for the transfer of his services and *corps d'armée* from the emperor to his successor; secondly, to escape the rough handling expected from the exasperated soldiers, who mutinied, and threatened him, when they became aware of his treachery and the object for which they were marched to Versailles surrounded by the Bavarian cavalry. They fired on their officers, shouted " *Vive l'empereur,*" and were with difficulty pacified.

A stipulation that "the person of Napoleon should not be sacrificed," as he termed it, should he fall into the hands of the allies, served as a soothing balm to the prickings of conscience which this traitor — the first of the marshals to desert — seems in some slight degree to have experienced.

The invisible authorities of Paris, as a polite attention to the enemy, had ordered the streets to be perfectly cleansed. They were nicely and

evenly sanded, too, in order that the rugged
paved roads on the line of march might less im-
pede the regular military step of the incoming
hosts.

As noon approached, a number of men of the
working class — the workshops and manufactories all being closed — began to appear in the
streets. There was then no sort of joyousness in
their manner, rather dejection. Curiosity probably drew them from their homes, and a desire to
see a grand military spectacle — always attractive
to the French. This one, they are told, is the
precursor of the much needed blessing of peace.
But that any display of the kind should take place
unconnected with some victory of their own great
captain, seems to most of them incredible — few
minds among the people being prepared to receive
as a fact that he could be brought so low and
utterly vanquished by those whom he so often
and so easily had conquered. The *chansonnier*
Béranger, who witnessed this scene, says : "The
people continually asked 'Where is he? Where
is he?'"

Paris generally that morning, but especially the
quartier St. Antoine, had been infested by a
set of noisy, idle vagrants in blouses, in twos and
threes, and sometimes as many as half a dozen
together. Having received a crown each for
using their lungs and exciting the people that
day, they rushed hither and thither brandishing

pieces of white calico, striving to multiply themselves by vociferous shouting and bawling at the
top of their voices : " Long live the allies !   Long
live the Bourbons ! Long live Louis XVIII.!
Down with Bonaparte !   Down with the Corsican
ogre ! " * Thus low had the mighty conqueror
already fallen !   All who listened to these fellows
were urged to "hasten to the *fête* of the kings,
and behold what real monarchs were like," ending
their story with a renewed shout of " Long live
the Bourbons ! "

"As well cry, 'Long live the dead !'" exclaimed one or two voices in reply; for the Bourbon race was believed by the people to have
become extinct in the persons of Louis XVI. and
the Duc d'Enghien.   The generation thus reminded of their existence were children of the
revolution and the empire.   They knew not the
Bourbons, except as an extirpated race of former
taskmasters, whose misrule had brought on
France and her people a long train of national
evils and family misfortunes.

But the tramp of the infantry is heard.   It
comes nearer, grows louder and louder.   Many
who had vowed that they would not bestow even
so much as a glance on these foreign foes cannot
now resist the impulse which bids them, as they
declare, "turn round and haughtily face them."

---

* An epithet first applied to him by the political pamphleteer,
Martainville, in an article in a journal of that morning.

Fond of the pomp and circumstance of war, they at once become interested spectators, and gaze with more of delight than haughtiness on the really grand military procession.   There are fifty thousand infantry of different nations passing along the boulevards.   They are followed by ten thousand cavalry and a train of artillery.   All are well equipped, and on the whole are a fairly good specimen of the sort of troops Napoleon's young soldiers have had to fight against.

As they defiled along the boulevards, Général Letort,* full of suppressed indignation, was waiting near the Madeleine to cross the road, when a voice behind him exclaimed : " *Pardieu !* these soldiers are men, not marionnettes like ours.   No wonder that such fine fellows should have given so thorough a dressing to our marmosets of conscripts."   The general turned fiercely round.   The speaker was a young man of good appearance.   He had a military air, and wore the red riband at his buttonhole.   " May I inquire," said the general, " if you are a Frenchman ? "   " I am," was the reply.   " And a military man, I presume ? "   " Yes," he answered, much astonished.   But the " yes " had scarcely passed his lips when the general's hand came with considerable force in contact with the

---

* He was then only colonel, but was promoted to the rank of general in 1815 by Napoleon, who also made him one of his aides-de-camp. He was killed on the 15th of June at the battle of Fleurus, while charging at the head of his squadrons.

side of his face. At the same time a card was
thrust into his hand, with the intimation that he
or any friend he might choose to send would find
the general at home any morning until twelve.
When the young man recovered from his amazement his assailant had disappeared. But "*le
lâche*," said the general, "never made his appearance to call me to an account for the insult he
had received. I ought," he would exclaim, working himself into a rage, when, as sometimes urged
by friends, he repeated the story, "I ought to
have killed him on the spot — yes, killed him, *le
lâche !*"

It was not, then, merely the mob who enjoyed
the spectacle of the march of an invading army
into the city, but equally volatile spectators of a
higher grade.

At the head of this army rode the Emperor
Alexander I. and the Grand Duke Constantine;
Frederick William III. of Prussia and his two
sons (one the present emperor); the commanders-
in-chief and a brilliant staff. The staff officers
wore on the left arm a white scarf or streamlet.
It was an emblem of victory. Many thought it
an announcement of peace; while the error that
the victors thus declared themselves champions
of the Bourbon cause was widely disseminated
by M. de Talleyrand and his emissaries — no less
actively, too, by that bevy of fair friends who so
zealously served him, whom he with infinite art

cajoled and flattered, and on whom he could always rely in matters requiring feminine acuteness and delicate subtlety to bring them to a happy issue.

It was owing to the untiring exertions of these fair devotees that Paris was so lavishly bedecked with white calico. The "pretty, serpent-faced Comtesse de Périgord," and her mother, the Duchesse de Courland, had urged all their acquaintances to make use of this cheap but effective decoration for the fronts of the balconies. Madame de Rémusat, whose ruse for keeping Talleyrand in Paris had succeeded so well,* was more than others eager in her desire to carry out her friends' views, and to contribute towards the overthrow of the man to whom she and her husband, like so many more of the traitorous band, owed everything.

Victory, peace, or the return of the Bourbons—any or all of these, according to the fancy of the wearer or spectator, were represented in white calico; whether fluttering on a pole, doing duty as a banner, draping the façade of a house, or traversing the brawny chests of some score or two of ill-looking ragamuffins—the most conspicuous, and apparently the most enthusiastic of the crowd. Calico, torn into strips, was also being deftly made up in cockades by the feminine circle assembled in the *salon* of the Hôtel Saint-Floren-

---

* See " *Mémoires de Madame la Duchesse d'Abrantès.*"

tin, where the Emperor Alexander's quarters were arranged, and from the windows of which the cockades descended on the crowd every few minutes like a shower of snowflakes. At each issue the Duc d'Alberg (a German by the way, and recently a groveller at the feet of his majesty the Emperor Napoleon, but now an opponent of "the Corsican Bonaparte," and of his claim to be a Frenchman) leaned forward and said aloud : " *On brentre les cocartes planches.*" This was to intimate to the laughing mob that they were expected to decorate themselves with the symbol of royalism thus graciously conferred on them.

All classes, however, seemed to be equally desirous of seeing the Emperor Alexander, and he certainly found immense favour with all. He was then thirty-six, but looked much younger, being tall, handsome, and fair, and of an elegant figure. As he passed the balconies, filled with ladies and children arrayed in white for the auspicious occasion, his graceful bow, recognised as "peculiarly French," at once conquered the hearts of these patriotic dames.   On all sides broke forth a chorus of admiration : "Ah ! what a handsome cavalier ! How graceful ! He really is charming ! adorable ! perfect ! "   No less graciously and gracefully did he acknowledge the acclamations of the people. They pressed so eagerly upon him that his escort found it difficult to keep the admiring mob at a sufficiently respectful distance, so persistently they strove to kiss the dusty boots of their so-called friend and saviour.

Doubtless enthusiasm is contagious; for after this sudden and exaggerated exhibition of it, all restraint seemed to vanish, and the joyous multitude gave themselves up to the hilarious celebration of their country's disgrace. That peaceably disposed monarch, Frederick William III., had met with but little attention at first from the spectators. But now a full tribute of applause is bestowed on him. It falls short of that paid to Alexander; but, as an eye-witness of this scene remarked: "However much his good Berliners may have loved him, he was never welcomed to his own capital with half so frantically joyous a greeting."

The levity and instability conspicuous in the French character could rarely have been more strikingly displayed than on the occasion in question. True, the excitement soon gave place to soberer feelings. Yet it seems almost incredible that people who began the day saddened by forebodings of evil should, in the space of an hour or two, by the very same event that caused their dejection, be worked up to a state of rapturous delight strongly resembling the intoxication of joy.

Perhaps the vigorous performance by the foreign bands of the inspiring airs, "*Vive Henri Quatre*" and "*Charmante Gabrielle*," had some

share in producing a temporary fever of excitement. The glorification of the loves of that gay
gallant and his beautiful mistress has always
played a prominent part in welcoming a new
ruler or government in France and the turning
out of a fallen one. Yet none but those swayed
by self-interest then dreamed of welcoming back
the Bourbons. Pride in the glories of the empire
may, however, have yielded before the satisfaction
that weary minds found in the near prospect held
out to them of a much needed and enduring
peace.

CHAPTER III.

"The City of Pleasure." — The Hetman Platoff. — The Deity of
the French Nation. — A Crowded Audience. — A Brilliant
Show. — "*Trajan*" and "*La Vestale*." — Their Majesties'
Modesty. — The Glorification of Henri IV. — A Doubtful
Compliment.

NO sooner were the ranks broken and
quarters assigned to the soldiers and
numerous officers of various grades
and various nations, most of whom now saw Paris
for the first time, than they thronged to the
public promenades, the Palais Royal cafés and
restaurants, and eagerly sought for the different
theatres. But the directors of these establishments had the decency to close their doors, at
least on the night of the 31st of March, and, on
the whole, the inhabitants of the "city of pleasure," which Paris was supposed to be, were not
so wholly given up to revelry as the rapturously
received invaders had expected, it seems, to find
them.

In default of theatrical and other entertainments, the foreign visitors amused themselves
by a raid on the wine stores. It was computed,
by one who was present, that not less than 65,000

or 70,000 bottles of champagne — that exhilarat-
ing beverage being more in request than any
other — were broached in honour of the auspicious day.   Disgraceful scenes of riot ensued
amongst the drunken foreign soldiery.   This led
to other depredations, tending further to diminish
their popularity, which had greatly waned since
the morning.

In every house several of these marauders were
quartered, and bed and board of the best, however grudgingly bestowed, must be provided for
them.   The ordinary fare of the Parisians did not
satisfy the ravenous appetites of "their friends
the enemy."   "No kickshaws for them.   The
mounseers must supply them with something far
more substantial," and quite unceremoniously they
demanded it.

The Duchesse d'Abrantès gives in her *Mémoires* an amusing account of the ample repasts
of the Hetman Platoff, and his Cossack officers,
who were quartered in the lower apartments of
the splendid hôtel she still inhabited in the
Champs-Élysées.   In the upper rooms of the
hôtel (which failure of means, consequent on
the downfall of Napoleon, compelled her ere long
to dispose of, together with the rich spoils of war
it contained, and all the art treasures collected by
Général Junot) Lord Cathcart and his staff were
lodged.   His influence with the ruling powers
soon relieved her of the unwelcome presence of

the Hetman, whose appetite caused immense annoyance to her *chef*. He declared that he could never succeed in appeasing it, however largely he prepared for and supplied it, or by any of his devices — devices which the duchess felt bound to condemn and forbid — create in the Don Cossacks or their chief the slightest loathing of food.

Paris at this time exhibited unusual scenes of drunkenness, riot, confusion, and general dissatisfaction. But, as the great Frederick once wrote to D'Alembert, "the deity of the French nation is novelty." The novelty, therefore, of much then surrounding them, together with the hope that a speedy peace would shortly relieve them of the presence of guests so barbarous, enabled the Parisians to bear up for awhile under troubles which the treacherous supineness of those left in charge of the capital had brought on them.

On the evening following the entry of the allies the theatres resumed their performances. Anxiety as to the result of the campaign had of late considerably diminished their receipts. The drooping spirits of the patriotic actors were therefore much cheered by the prospect of full houses after performing so many nights to "a beggarly account of empty boxes." But again they sank when it was bruited about that the newcomers looked to be amused at the theatres and elsewhere gratuitously. This pretension, however, was at once disallowed by an imperative mandate from head-

quarters. Consequently, money was then forthcoming, and enough to fill all the theatres to
overflowing — *florins*, *guineas*, and *ducats* stream-
ing in in abundance and replenishing their empty
treasuries.

But it was at the Opera-house on the 1st of
April where Parisians and foreigners assembled in
greatest force. There Alexander and Frederick
William were expected to be present. The house
was packed stiflingly full from floor to ceiling
almost immediately after the doors were opened.
As many more spectators would have effected an
entry had it been possible. As it was not, not an
inch even of standing-room being available, they
congregated in a dense mass in the Rue de Richelieu — forming an obstacle to the passing of a
line of carriages, filled with elegantly dressed
ladies for whom places were reserved, but whom
the swaying crowd for a considerable time prevented from approaching the entrances.

The theatre presented a brilliant show of rich
and dazzling uniforms, to which greater effect was
given by the ladies' white dresses, waving white
plumes, fluttering white fans, lilies, pearls, and
diamonds. There was a fair sprinkling, too, of
Saint-Florentin cockades, though probably very
few indicated that the wearers were really partisans
of the "right divine." The French are prone to
yield when strong pressure is put on them, and
war's alarms at the gates of Paris produced in

many breasts — as some French writers assert — results that in others were due to royalist principles only. It was, however, remarked that the foreign element predominated amongst the male portion of the audience; and those who had waited for hours for the opening of the doors complained loudly of so many favoured individuals having been privately admitted before the public were allowed to enter.

But the audience is becoming impatient, the French part of it at least, for the royalties are tardy in making their appearance. The orchestra, obedient to the demand of the people, have played "*Henri Quatre*," and of course the inseparable "*Charmante Gabrielle*," with great spirit as often as the many encores received have compelled them to renew these favourite and so-called monarchical airs. Yet the mighty potentates still are absent. Murmurs are beginning to be heard, when the actor Dérevis steps before the curtain and explains that the sudden indisposition of a principal performer makes it necessary to change the piece announced for that of "*La Vestale*." Many of the audience vehemently protest against this new arrangement, and declare that the opera of "*Trajan*" only will they listen to.

This opera, composed expressly to glorify Napoleon and his victories over the Russians and Prussians, was, strangely enough, chosen by the administration of the Opera-house — perhaps as

a sort of malicious pleasantry — for the occasion
of the visit of the allied sovereigns. The fulsome
flattery so lavishly heaped on the fallen hero at
the height of his power and glory was to be transferred, for the nonce, to his triumphant foes.
But the determination on the part of the audience
to accept no substitute for " *Trajan* " evoked the
real cause of the delay of the sovereigns in making their appearance. It was the refusal of their
majesties to accept the laudatory and flattering
allusions contained in the opera selected for
their visit.

Dérevis again comes forward to make this
announcement of their majesties' modesty, and to
say that the Emperor of Russia has expressed
his own and the king's willingness to honour by
their presence the performance of " *La Vestale.*"
The actor appeals to the " good sense " of the
audience, and at once the imperial decision is
deferentially bowed to. Alexander and Frederick
William enter together, and take their seats in
the imperial box surmounted by the eagles of
France. The whole house rises. Deafening
acclamations greet them. But they make their
acknowledgments with some constraint, even embarrassment, as though they feel this exuberant
expression of joy to be far in excess of what the
occasion requires.

When, after this jubilant welcome, calmness is
in some degree restored, the performers appear

and "*La Vestale*" commences. But so little attention does it receive from the audience that none seem to be aware that it is given with the scenery of "*Trajan.*" On ordinary occasions this would neither have escaped notice nor noisy remonstrances. But the object of this brilliant *réunion* was rather to *fête* the royal, though unbidden, guests than to listen to an operatic performance. Often indeed it was interrupted, and "*La Vestale*" herself required to sing the praises of the gallant Henri and his mistress, the whole house joining with the rest of the performers in the chorus. Both invaders and invaded in the warmth of their enthusiasm vociferated until they were hoarse, and the evening terminated with much emotional pressing of hands and fervent embracing.

All the theatres in turn were honoured by the visits of the allied sovereigns; the souvenirs attaching to Henri IV. forming the usual theme of the pieces represented. "*Le Souper de Henri Quatre,*" "*Les Clefs de Paris,*" were chief favourites; while every one was sent into ecstasies when, with electrifying spirit, the orchestra struck up the eternal strains of "*Vive Henri Quatre*" and "*Charmante Gabrielle.*" "The most devout ladies," says M. Murat, "were overwhelmed with delight while listening to the glorification of the roystering *vert-galant* and his *belle maîtresse.* Paris resounded with these supposed monarchical songs ; and nothing better, in the estimation of all classes, could be found to welcome back the decendant of Saint Louis to his kingdom.

" The orchestra of the Opera-house and of the theatres generally, the little street organs, the tinkling pianos of private *salons*, were all unceasingly employed in celebrating the loves of Henri and his Gabrielle, in compliment to the returning Bourbons. Probably it was intended thus to announce that the privileges of royal personages were universal ; that the morality of ordinary human beings was no standard for them any more than it had been for Jupiter and the Olympian deities. Or, perhaps, the generous and magnanimous qualities of the great Henri were left unsung, as having perished with him ; while his vices, which alone survived in his descendants, were the only remaining traits of resemblance between the popular monarch and his successors." *

* *L'histoire par le Théâtre.*

CHAPTER IV.

THE language of the morrow was but little in harmony with the sentimental enthusiasm displayed with such seeming unanimity at the opera *fête*. The majority of the *bourgeoisie* had no sympathy with those extravagant demonstrations of feeling. Many, too, who had joined in the songs and vociferous acclamations at the theatres, now regarded the position of affairs from a soberer point of view. For during the night the walls of Paris had been covered with a proclamation which, in the name of the Emperor Alexander, promised more favourable terms of peace to France because of her return to a wise government.

This puzzled the people, and they anxiously inquired what this wise form of government might be.

The royalist committee had been active in propagating monarchical ideas by means of pamphlets, songs, and caricatures; which, though failing in their aim to imbue the public mind with monarchical sentiments, yet had already succeeded in making the actual existence of the Bourbons a recognised fact, even by the dullest and most ignorant. But the Russian emperor — whether M. de Talleyrand had or had not succeeded in convincing him that " Louis XVIII. was a principle," for the consecration of which the allies had fought — had not thought it needful to make any public declaration of his wishes respecting the Bourbon family. He, however, was believed to be opposed to their restoration, and inclined to favour the elevation of Bernadotte to the throne of Napoleon.

Again, it was whispered about that the partisans of the younger branch, already on the *qui vive*, had secretly suggested the Duc d'Orléans as a desirable constitutional king, and that Alexander had turned no unwilling ear to them. In a word, he was supposed to be coquetting with all parties, while maintaining the most amiable relations with the princely host of the Hôtel Saint-Florentin, who entertained him and his suite right royally.*

But on the 2d of April many conjectures were set at rest, many illusions dispelled. For on that eventful day the Senate concluded its *séance* with a declaration that, "Napoleon having deserted

* Private letters of 1814.

them, they felt themselves authorised to make choice of another chief for the government of France. Consequently, as with one voice, they called their legitimate sovereign, Louis XVIII., to the throne of his ancestors." A provisional government was appointed to guide the vessel of the state *ad interim* — M. de Talleyrand helmsman; the officers and crew his humble servants. The duty of elaborating a new constitution "in conformity with the needs and the wishes of the nation" was assigned them. It was to be presented to the restored monarch on his arrival, and M. de Talleyrand guaranteed its acceptance.

On the same day appeared M. de Châteaubriand's famous pamphlet, " *De Bonaparte et des Bourbons,*" etc. In it the great French writer condescends to employ the language of insult and calumny, and to designate the fallen warrior-chief by such contemptuous epithets as " *histrion, comédien* — a mere stage king, in fact. Yet in 1802 he dedicated to him, as "the restorer of religion," his " *Génie du Christianisme.*" Soon after, he was attached to the Roman embassy, through the interest of Lucien Bonaparte and his sister Madame Bacciochi; both of whom showed much kindness to M. de Châteaubriand when, as a returning emigrant, he came back to France in poverty. Subsequently the First Consul appointed him French minister to the republic of Valais. But the sad catastrophe of the Duc d'Enghien's

arrest and execution induced him to resign, and
to separate himself from the government of
Napoleon.

It has, however, been frequently asserted that
Napoleon, at any time during his reign, might
have bought the chevalier's facile and influential
pen, had he chosen to flatter him and pay for his
services the very high price which his excessive
egotism led him to set on them. The emperor
always declared that the difficulty was not in buy-
ing M. de Châteaubriand, but in paying the sum
at which he estimated himself. His pamphlet,
which was widely distributed, doubtless did good
service to the Bourbon cause. When the author
was presented to Louis XVIII., on his arrival at
Compiègne, the king declared, with flattering exaggeration, which, as he knew the man, he knew
would please, that 100,000 soldiers would have
given him less valuable aid than he had derived
from M. de Châteaubriand's forcible and eloquently
expressed arguments. If it was so, then the
pamphlet was but scantily recompensed by elevation to the peerage and a grant of 20,000
francs. For this sum the chevalier's name figured
on the list of recipients of the king's bounty when
a portion of the imperial treasure in the vaults of
the Tuileries was divided amongst the ravenous
shoals of returning emigrants.

Whilst the Restoration was proceeding at a
rapid pace in Paris, Napoleon remained at Fon-

tainebleau in a meditative mood, mistaken by some of those about him for resignation — resignation to fate's decree, that his career of glory was ended. Yet he had with him 50,000 soldiers devoted to him, and burning to avenge the shame of the capitulation. But Napoleon was aware that no such ardour animated his marshals. *They* urged on him the necessity of signing an act of abdication, in order to avert the miseries of civil war, and to preserve the throne for his son. M. de Caulaincourt had arrived from Paris on the evening of the 2d, to announce the refusal of the allies to treat with Napoleon. They demanded his abdication. That alone would satisfy his so recently obsequious Senate, now the self-elected provisional government.

Indignant at these pretensions, he laid before his marshals a plan he had formed for marching on Paris conjointly with the corps of the Ducs de Ragusa and Trévise (Marmont and Mortier). But the once intrepid lieutenants of the army of Italy listened to their chief in silence. They are now the great dignitaries of that crumbling empire they had helped to build up ; but in its fall they have no desire to share. Wealth and honours have been heaped on them. To retain them they scruple not to desert in his hour of adversity the man who conferred them. Already Marmont's defection is not an isolated instance of abandonment of duty for the sake of personal interests.

The Ducs de Valmy and Bellune (Maréchaux Victor and Kellermann), with Général Nansouty and others, have discarded the *tricolor*, as dear to the old republicans as to the Bonapartists, and adopted the white cockade.

"This sort of treachery," says a private letter, "excites strong feelings of contempt even amongst the party that is to be the gainer by it, and is loudly inveighed against by men who are not the warmest of Bonaparte's partisans." Others, again, look wise and whisper : " These men are no traitors. They have taken the only way now open to them of serving their chief, and may be called a corps of generals in reserve. The idea doubtless prevails that the end is not yet, but on what it is founded does not clearly appear."

Napoleon, however, perceives that he can no longer rely on his marshals. In much bitterness of spirit, and after some hesitation, he writes and signs his abdication. But it is in favour of his son, under the regency of Maria Louisa.

M. de Caulaincourt was deputed to bear this document to Paris. Maréchaux Oudinot, Ney, and Macdonald accompanied him ; and it was the wish of Napoleon that Marmont, of whom he had a high opinion, should join them. At Essone they unexpectedly met with him. Great was the marshal's consternation, and so great his fears lest his own private negotiation with the enemy should be affected by M. de Caulaincourt's mission, that he acknowledged having made certain proposals to Prince Schwarzenberg, the sole motive of which, he declared, was the good of the State. But Napoleon's plenipotentiaries, indignant at the marshal's presumption in treating with the enemy separately and on his own account, were disposed to arrest him. They, however, contented themselves with sending off a message to the emperor, informing him that Marmont had gone over to the allies. In an order of the day his treason was denounced to the army of Fontainebleau, whose indignation was expressed in no measured terms.

On the evening of the 4th, the Duc de Vicenza and the marshals arrived at the Hôtel Saint-Florentin. Before they were allowed to see the Emperor Alexander, Prince Talleyrand received them in his *salon*, that he might expostulate with and reproach them. "Gentlemen," he said, "what is this you would do? Are you not aware that if you succeed in proclaiming the regency, you compromise all who have entered this room since the 1st of April? The number, I assure you, is not a small one. I include not myself. I would wish to be compromised." What this expression was intended to convey, he alone probably knew.

Admitted to the presence of the Russian emperor, they laid Napoleon's abdication before him, and demanded the regency in the name of the army. Much inquietude of mind prevailed that

evening among the numerous guests who passed
restlessly in and out of the Hôtel Saint-Florentin
while this interview with Alexander lasted. It
was comparatively a long interview, from which
many of the royalists were disposed to forebode
evil. M. de Talleyrand had not been summoned
to give his advice or opinion. He knew that the
emperor had a wavering mind, and might be
drawn by M. de Caulaincourt, for whom he had
a liking, into making some promise which, although it might not be kept, yet in the present
position of affairs would prove embarrassing.

But Alexander, with whom all arrangements
respecting the future form of government in
France appear to have rested, was as prudent as
M. de Talleyrand himself could have been. Reminded that he had said that "the allies came not
to France to impose on the nation a ruler or a
government," he assented, and listened with com-
plaisance to the reasons adduced in favour of
Napoleon II. and the regency. However, Général
Dessoles, an enemy on whom Napoleon had
heaped many favours, being in the cabinet,—
either as secretary or aide-de-camp, for the time
being, to Alexander,— ventured to say, "The regency, sire, would be only Bonaparte in disguise."

The duke and the marshals retorted with
asperity, and the emperor at once put an end to
the interview, observing that on so important a
matter he must necessarily consult the King of

Prussia, and would communicate to them the result. This communication was anxiously awaited at Maréchal Ney's. It was a demand for a fresh abdication, absolute, not only as regarded Napoleon himself, but his son and the whole of the Bonaparte family. Had the Emperor of Austria and Prince Metternich been in Paris at this moment, they, probably, would have supported the claims of Napoleon II. and regency of Maria Louisa, for many preferred the regency to the Bourbons. But Francis and his minister lingered at Dijon, and lost their opportunity. Napoleon indignantly refused compliance with this new demand, and began to enumerate the resources which yet remained to him in the North, the South, the Alps, etc., with a view of renewing the war. But this project found no adherents. The countenances of his old comrades, as they listened to him, became more and more clouded, and they replied to his appeals only by objections. " Had he then," says Baron Fain, " but left these hereditary dukes of the empire and passed into the room of the secondary officers, he would have found young and enthusiastic men eager to follow him. A few steps further, and he would have been saluted by his soldiers with acclamations whose warmth would have reanimated his drooping spirit, and called forth anew his wonted vigour and activity of mind. A squadron of the imperial guard, dashing into Paris to the cry of '*Vive*

l'empereur!' would have roused the whole population, who would have rallied to his standard to
a man."

Such a result, to say the least, was at that
particular juncture very doubtful. For there was
a longing for peace. It was felt by all to be the
great need of the nation. But the position of
Napoleon was humiliating in the extreme, and it
was scarcely possible that he, so recently at the
height of power and glory, should without a
terrible mental struggle bow to it. He displayed
some irritation at the apathy, as he considered,
with which the marshals regarded the dishonour
of the capitulation, and spoke with bitter sarcasm
of the conduct of the Senate, who, when, little
more than two months before, he took leave of
them to open the campaign, would have licked the
dust from his feet. Nevertheless, after some
moments of reflection, yielding to circumstances,
he silently took up a pen, wrote what the allies
had demanded, and, without remark, handed the
document to the Duc de Vicenza, who forthwith
proceeded with it to Paris.

While waiting for precise information respecting
the " honourable and independent existence promised by Alexander to Napoleon in the name of
the allies, and which was to be in every way
befitting the elevated position the fallen hero has
held in Europe," Talleyrand invites the emperor's
envoy to join the provisional government. He

knows that M. de Caulaincourt is a man of ability. He is mortified to find that, unlike himself, he is also a man of integrity, who cannot be seduced to desert the master he has served so long because adverse fate has overtaken him.

Alexander and his cabinet council fluctuated for a time in their choice of a residence for Napoleon. Corfu, Corsica, Ferreira, and Elba were severally proposed, the preference being given to Elba, until he could be transferred to the prison England had in reserve for him. The Czar afterwards conferred with the marshals, individually and collectively, and having gained over Macdonald to his views, Marmont and one or two others being already secured, it was determined to offer Napoleon the island of Elba "for a retreat." A revenue of six million *francs* was proposed — three for himself and Maria Louisa, and three as a provision for his brothers and sisters. His retention of the title of emperor was also conceded. But M. de Caulaincourt and Maréchal Ney vehemently opposed this arrangement, and again urged the appointment of a regency. Alexander, however, was firm, repeating the determination of the allies not to treat with Napoleon.

A private letter from Paris of the 7th says: "The great drama is ended. Bonaparte's answer was awaited here by the ruling powers with intensest anxiety, which, under present circumstances, would to most persons seem singular.

The truth is, the army cannot be trusted. To abandon the *tricolor*, with its associations of liberty and glory, for the white flag and white cockade,* is to many regiments, both officers and men, a very sore trial indeed. A signal from one, whom even Talleyrand acknowledges to be the 'first soldier in the world,' would at this moment certainly cause a great commotion, and possibly something more. But Maréchal Ney has written that Bonaparte accepts a residence at Elba, and desires that his wife and son may rejoin him without delay. About this, however, there is some doubt."

After reading the treaty conferring on him the *sovereignty* of Elba, with pensions to himself and his brothers and sisters, Napoleon took offence at the pretension of the allies to regulate, as he said, "the destiny of every member of his family," and refused to sign it. A courier was sent after M. de Caulaincourt to order the withdrawal of his abdication. But it was too late. The allies or their representatives had signed the treaty on the 11th. His messenger further informed him that the Comte d'Artois entered Paris on the 12th, and that the empress and his son would not be permitted to join him, or even to bid him adieu.

Maria Louisa was utterly wanting in decision of character, therefore quite unequal to sustaining

* A decree of the 9th abolished the former and reëstablished the latter.

the part of heroine, as she had then an opportunity of doing. Duty pointed one way, inclination drew her another. Full of perplexity, she placed herself under the protection and guidance of the allies, and was very readily detached from the interests of her husband and son, and of her adopted country.

"Nearly all Napoleon's princes and dukes," the letter above quoted continues, "have forsaken him. Even Berthier, they say, after biting his nails to the quick until they ran blood, — apparently under the influence of some strong feeling that for a while held him back, — has overcome his hesitation, and, following the example of others, proved faithless at the last. It remains to be seen how these men and the people generally will like their most Christian king when they get him. We, however, very much doubt whether those who are to succeed the fallen giant are likely, with their base intrigues, restless ambition, and personal animosities, — already but too apparent, — to restore peace and prosperity to France."

The many afflicting and humiliating circumstances with which it was sought to embitter the fall of Napoleon, together with the almost total abandonment and solitude in which he felt himself at Fontainebleau, produced in him the most poignant mental anguish. Reacting on his already unstrung constitution, it resulted, on the night of the 14th of April, in that intense bodily suffering

which has been sometimes ascribed to poison.
Failing, it has been asserted, to find the relief he
sought in death, he whispered to M. de Caulaincourt — who, with Count Bertrand and the Duc
de Bassano, was then staying at the palace —
" God does not wish it." M. de Caulaincourt,
however, denied this, as did his other two friends,
who were present also. They attributed his sufferings on that mysterious night solely to a paroxysm
of intense agony of mind reacting on the body.

On the morrow, greater resignation to his fate
was the only change observable in him. He asked
for the treaty (the treaty of Fontainebleau) which
he had rejected, and at once signed it. It grati-
fied him to hear that Maréchal Soult had success-
fully attacked Lord Wellington at Toulouse on
the 10th, as it confirmed him in his conviction
that he might have implicitly relied on his army
had he resumed hostilities, and even have still
placed confidence in some of his generals. It may
have been also a cheering conviction held in reserve for the future. He knew not yet of Augereau's base conduct at Lyons, and the insulting
proclamation in which he made known to the
troops the downfall of their chief.

The allies now announced that Napoleon was
free to depart. Four commissioners, representing
Russia, Austria, Prussia, and England, with a
small escort, were to accompany him. At noon
on the 20th of April the old guard was drawn up

Napolcon.
Photo-etching after the painting by Robert Le Fèvre.

in the court of honour. Napoleon, wearing a general's uniform, with the historical gray overcoat and three-cornered hat, soon after appeared on the grand terrace. Slowly he descended the steps and passed along the lines of his old companions in arms. His address and his adieux to these scarred and weather-beaten soldiers were alike solemn, touching, and dignified. They were listened to with deep emotion, and he was himself much affected, his voice losing firmness as he uttered his last words — "*Adieu, mes enfants ! Mes vœux vous accompagneront toujours !*"

It was the will of M. de Talleyrand and his royalist accomplices that one continued demonstration of hatred and hostile feeling should attend Napoleon on his journey to Fréjus, and no pains were spared by their emissaries to incite the people to insult him. This was meant, probably, to justify his assassination, which Baron Maubreuil was commissioned to find means of accomplishing. So, at least, he persistently declared in the face of Europe, and to the face of M. de Talleyrand himself. That he was officially charged to waylay the princess of Bavaria, Jérôme Bonaparte's wife, in the forest of Fontainebleau, and rob her of her money and jewels, is well known ; also that he did it effectually and to the satisfaction of his princely employers.*

---

* It was this same Baron Maubreuil whom the provisional government commissioned to recruit soldiers for the army of

However, in spite of all efforts to raise a contrary cry, " *Vive l'empereur !* " resounded through every town and village on the road, even to the frontiers of Provence. The assassin found no opportunity of unsheathing his dagger, or he may have recoiled from the dark deed, and thus Elba was reached in safety. Avignon was certainly avoided, — a city which, but a year later, obtained the unenviable notoriety of being the scene of murder and crime more horrible, more revolting and cruel than any of the sanguinary deeds of the Reign of Terror.

Several detachments of Maréchal Augereau's corps were met on the road returning from Lyons. They saluted their emperor with the customary honours, cheered him with enthusiasm, and

---

the Restoration. For five days his headquarters were in the Place Vendôme, where the most disgraceful scenes occurred — none perhaps more disgraceful than the attempt of a mob of ragged ruffians (Bourbon *sans-culottes*) to overthrow the statue of Napoleon. The attempt proving unsuccessful, a number of young men of noble family, — the sons of returned emigrants, — to prove their hatred of the "usurper," harnessed themselves together with these vagrants like a gang of convicts, and, a rope being put round the neck of the statue, did their best to pull it from the summit of the column raised to the glory of the French arms. Vain were all their efforts, happily, probably, for themselves. However, these zealous royalists were resolved that the statue should fall with the hero it represented. Delauney, its founder, was therefore sought, and, under pain of military execution, was ordered by Count Rochechouart to take down the statue, in expiation of the crime of having so firmly fixed it on its lofty pedestal. — ANQUETIL.

shouted : " Sire, Maréchal Augereau has sold your army."

On the 3d of May he anchored in the roadstead of Porto Ferrigo, and was received with a salute of 101 guns. On the 4th he landed. The whole population of his islet empire, headed by the municipality and the clergy, had assembled to greet him with joyous acclamations expressive of their good-will and gladness

CHAPTER V.

WHILE preparations were making at Fontainebleau for the departure of Napoleon, the Bourbons singly and at short
intervals made their appearance in Paris. Louis
XVIII. was still at Hartwell, unable, in fact, to
leave it. He was suffering from the reaction
caused by the realisation of hope deferred. So
much was he overwhelmed with delight when, on
the 5th of April, he was informed that the throne
of France, which for so many years he had sighed
to sit on, and for which he so unscrupulously had
sought to displace his brother, was vacant for him,
that he was near losing the enjoyment of this
cherished wish of his heart by intense nervous
emotion at the moment of its fulfilment. Several

days elapsed before his favourite medical attendant, le Père Élisée, thought him sufficiently calmed
down to set out for that France to which M. de
Talleyrand so obsequiously invited him, as the
"well-beloved of the nation; the long-desired monarch whose return was so yearned for, and who
was so earnestly prayed to come quickly."

"Fine words!" exclaimed the king. But he
put not the smallest faith in them; for, as Cardinal Maury said, "the Comte de Provence knew
the Bishop of Autun well, and was more *rusé*
even than he."

The first of the family to present himself to the
longing eyes of the Parisians was the Comte
d'Artois, self-created lieutenant-general of the
kingdom. M. de Talleyrand, however, suggested
his being welcomed to Paris as Monsieur — the
title always borne by the king's eldest brother
under the old *régime*. On the 12th of April, a
charming spring day, he arrived at the barrier of
Bondy, attended by a numerous retinue of royalist emigrants and several priests, and escorted by a
detachment of troops from Lord Wellington's
army. He and his son, the Duc d'Angoulême,
had been staying for protection at the English
headquarters in the South, while awaiting M. de
Talleyrand's signal to enter the capital.

The members of the provisional government
went in a body to receive him. M. de Talleyrand,
being their president, was also their spokesman.

In his most winning manner he begged Monsieur to " condescend, with that celestial goodness which had ever characterised his illustrious house, to accept his and his colleagues' homage of religious attachment and respectful devotion." The count bowed and smiled, then stammered out in reply some few unconnected, unintelligible words, from which none could gather any meaning. But Talleyrand, knowing that Monsieur was not gifted with an eloquent tongue, came to his rescue, and, purposely, the rest of his mutterings were lost in an enthusiastic outburst of loyal *vivas*.

How it must have surprised Monsieur, if he looked at the *Moniteur* of the following morning, to find that all unconsciously he had really made a *spirituel* reply to M. de Talleyrand's address : " Once more I behold fair France. Nothing is changed there, unless it be that it contains one more Frenchman ! " But alas ! he was not so well inspired. It was but the happy thought of M. de Beugnot, the editor, who, consulting with his editorial colleagues, declared that " it would not do to report the Comte d'Artois's entry into Paris without attributing a speech of some sort to him." The above brief and telling phrase, by many considered " charmingly " patriotic, occurred at that moment to M. de Beugnot. It was at once adopted and sent forth to the world as spoken by Monsieur. This seemed very like a promise to those who were in the secret, and the promise undoubtedly was realised, that the epithet " *Menteur,*" so long applied to the *Moniteur* under the imperial *régime*, would be a no less appropriate appellation under the new order of things.

Besides the members of the provisional government, a cavalcade of between two and three hundred royalist gentlemen rode out to the barrier to greet Monsieur on his return to the land of his birth. The Chevalier de Châteaubriand was one of them, and was especially presented to him. A copy of the famous pamphlet was at the same time handed to Monsieur, and a hope expressed that he would condescend to honour its author by reading it. "Otherwise," says the astonished chevalier, in his " *Mémoires d'outre-tombe,*" " he would not have recollected my name. For he had no idea of having seen me at the Court of Louis XVI., or at the camp of Thionville, and doubtless had never heard of the ' *Génie du Christianisme* ' ! "

What a blow this must have been to the vanity of M. de Châteaubriand, who was a fluent, poetic, and able writer, but believed himself to be the greatest genius of that age, and universally known and accepted as such. But then, Monsieur was no reader, and had not the wonderful memory with which his elder brother, Louis XVIII., was gifted — a memory that enabled him to recognise at any distance of time a person whom he had once seen, and, though his attainments were shallow, to dazzle, with his endless quotations from Latin authors, those who were not profound scholars themselves, by seeming to possess all learning and all knowledge.

But when Monsieur was made to comprehend that this Chevalier de Châteaubriand's pamphlet contained much eloquent abuse of the "Corsican usurper," and, as might have been added, equally eloquent and untruthful praise of the Bourbons, he bowed with his accustomed infinite grace, and blandly smiled his approval. His great forte, as every one knew, lay in bowing and smiling ; but his capacity for treating of the affairs of the kingdom which now devolved on him in the post to which he had appointed himself, was expressed by the phrase that he had no more brains than a hare. His mother, the Princess of Saxony, was distinguished among the ladies of the court for her graceful bowing and daring riding. The count alone of her family inherited her grace and equestrian skill.

His indifference to the public feeling was shown on the occasion in question by his wearing the military hat or cap called the "*petit chapeau à la Wellington,*" and otherwise affecting the Englishman in his dress. The national guard, drawn up at the barrier, and deputed to escort him thence into Paris, took great offence at this glaring indiscretion. Already much aggrieved by the arbitrary

and impolitic substitution of the white cockade
and banner for the long cherished *tricolor*, they
expressed their disapprobation in loud and angry
murmurs. But the lieutenant-general's gross mistake was adroitly turned to his advantage by a
member of the provisional government whose
château was in the vicinity. Very humbly he
requested that Monsieur would do him the honour
to rest there awhile before entering the capital,
and his request was condescendingly complied
with.

After a short interval Monsieur reappeared. To
the astonishment of the citizen soldiers he wore
the uniform of a colonel of the national guard.
Presumably it had been provided for him, and M.
de Talleyrand may have done him that service.
His forethought and foresight were certainly as
remarkable as his activity in smoothing the path
for the returning Bourbons. *Vivas* loud and long
now greeted the count, for many of the guard
were simple enough to believe that he had retired
to make the change in compliment to them, as his
new escort. They were therefore as overanxious
to applaud as they considered they had been over-
hasty to murmur.

The Comte d'Artois's " prudent and politic act "
was reported in Paris, and much credit awarded
him in consequence ; while the constitutional
party's hopes and expectations for the future ran
high, based on this slightest of foundations. It

would never have occurred to the Comte d'Artois to be guilty of such a concession to the feelings or prejudices of the people, if those who knew better than he the real state of public opinion in Paris had not counselled the change, and impressed on him its importance and necessity.*

The old dowagers of the Faubourg St. Germain, who had contrived to exist in France during the revolution, or had returned to it when Bonaparte became First Consul (though neither of these was favourably received, if tolerated, at the court of the Restoration), were in ecstasies at the arrival of their "Galaor," as they called him, the "*vrai chevalier français.*" This gay gallant — the insolent, arrogant *roué* of the depraved court of their early days, when the misguided Marie Antoinette was queen — would prove, they prophesied, a formidable rival to the popular emperor.

During the ten or twelve days that the allies had occupied Paris, Alexander was said to have conquered the capital on his own account. He had acquired such a reputation for wisdom as to be named the "Solomon of the North." All classes looked up to him, and he was popular even with the army. The Parisians accepted him as their king — at least in a political sense, and while waiting the arrival of Louis XVIII., another Solomon, no less "*fin, faux, et adroit*" (to quote Napoleon's words) than he.

* Private letters of 1814 and 1815.

Alexander I. of Russia.
Photo-etching from a rare print.

But this all-conquering Russian czar reigned also with absolute sway as king of hearts in the *salons*, whether presided over by ladies of the old or the imperial *régime*. It was suspected that he preferred the latter, as he was so frequent a visitor in the Rue Ceruti at the hôtel of Queen Hortense. But there, or elsewhere, form and ceremony were dispensed with as much as possible in compliance with his wish; he setting the example by his own great affability. His manners were fascinating, "adorable," as the ladies in chorus continued to exclaim whenever he was mentioned. Courteous and gallant towards all, both old and young, he undoubtedly was, and perhaps something more than that towards one or two whom he especially delighted to honour.

Alexander, however, was young — several years younger than the Comte d'Artois's elder son, the Duc d'Angoulême. And besides that, the count, once "the glass of fashion and mould of form," was now verging on sixty, and a dissipated life, together with the ordinary results of the withering hand of time, had wrought a very marked change in him personally; a change no less marked had come over him in spirit — the *débauché* had become a devotee!

His last *maîtresse-en-titre*, the Marquise de Polastron, whom an illness had carried off prematurely, repented of the irregularities of her life when on her death-bed. Having thus, as she believed, made her peace with heaven, and secured happiness in the next world when compelled to renounce the pleasures of this, she implored "her Charles" to follow her pious example. Then, though for a brief space they must be separated, they would meet again, and the *liaison* which the Fates so cruelly severed in this world would be happily and lastingly renewed in the next.

Charles complied with the request of his marquise. He abstained from riotous living, confessed, and received absolution. Time indeed it was, that one who had already reached the sere-and-yellow-leaf stage of life should cease to sow wild oats. From the arms of his mistress, then, he rushed into the arms of the Jesuits, by whom he had been brought up, and who received with gladness their repentant prodigal son.

He did not proclaim, like his great ancestor Henri IV., when death snatched from him his charming Gabrielle, that "his heart was cold and dead to love, even to its very root, so that the tender passion could never again live and flourish there." Yet it was generally whispered about that, as in the case of that gallant monarch, who, after a short season devoted to sadness and mourning, discovered that a corner of his heart had escaped·the withering blight he supposed had fallen wholly upon it, so it had happened with the gay Comte d'Artois, now the pious Monsieur. However, no recognised *maîtresse - en - titre* had hitherto succeeded the Marquise de Polastron. And as that high office had been abolished in France — at least in name — ever since the time of Madame du Barry, it was probably not one of the many projected revivals of the usages and customs of the good old Bourbon days.

Monsieur was welcomed to Paris with joyous acclamations by the royalists, both old and new, and by the Parisian public with keen curiosity. The French have a weakness for a graceful *tournure*. And as the Comte d'Artois, notwithstanding his worn, expressionless countenance, was still in personal appearance the most presentable of his family, it was well that he should be seen of the people first. He was an excellent horseman, bowed gracefully, smiled pleasantly, if somewhat simperingly, when he was pleased, and bore himself with that air of *grand seigneur*, supposed to be the special attribute of high birth and breeding under the old *régime*.

Early in the day he attended mass at Notre-Dame, where a *Te Deum* and *Domine Salvum* were given with grand orchestral accompaniments. The church was thronged with ladies, who of course were much affected by the sanctimonious earnestness with which their prince bore a part in the service. Afterwards he took possession of the Tuileries in the name of Louis XVIII. There, even he must have been startled by the change. In that ancient royal residence, abandoned by the Bourbons, all now was splendour, where, when Louis XVI. and his queen, driven from Versailles to Paris by the insurgent mob, were compelled to reside in it, they found only bare walls to shelter them, a bed and a few chairs being borrowed for the night of their arrival. In the evening the provisional government gave a ball, which the Comte d'Artois graced by his presence, smiling and bowing indefatigably, and appearing to be guileless as a dove, if not as wise as a serpent.

The Duc d'Angoulême — a second Saint Louis, according to royalist reports — had entered Bordeaux under the fostering wing of Maréchal Beresford, and there proclaimed Louis XVIII. While awaiting orders to proceed to Paris, he was wandering from village to village and town to town, to accustom the people, he said, to the presence of their legitimate princes.

His brother, the Duc de Berry, had a less saintly reputation. He was more given, like his father in his youth, to worldly pleasures and making love to *les belles* than to mass and confession. France was therefore told to expect in him another Henri IV.

For some weeks he had been waiting in Jersey, in anxious expectation of the result of the campaign. On the 14th he landed at Cherbourg, provided by Louis XVIII. with a set of harangues to be spoken to the people of Rouen and other towns on his route to Paris. His oratory made an unfavourable impression, the burden of his message being, " Frenchmen, we return to you, forgetting the wrongs of the unfortunate past!" Having blurted this out, as though under the influence of strong emotion, he melted into tears and sank on the breast of any one of the authorities of the town who chanced to be nearest to him.

All this was regarded as an amusing farce; even Napoleon's renegade marshals sneered at his seemingly irrepressible emotion when, on being presented to him, he rushed into their arms, embraced them severally, and in gasping utterances expressed an earnest wish that his sentiments of affection towards them might be reciprocated. The duke's promenade from Cherbourg to Paris was accomplished very leisurely; in all probability that he might not divide honours with Francis II. and his minister Count Metternich, who reached Paris a few days before the valiant Duc de Berry.

The Emperor of Austria's entry into Paris was a very grand *spectacle*, — a great display of military pomp, all the troops of the allied armies lining the streets and boulevards on either side along the route taken by the procession. To give greater effect to it, vehicles of every kind were prohibited from passing to and fro, and all were invited to add to the splendour of the triumphal march of the modest Emperor Francis by decorating the fronts of the houses.   Flags of all nations were available for mingling with the white calico that represented France.   The *tricolor* only was proscribed.   Though so dear to the hearts of the people, it was no longer their national flag.   It was, therefore, put out of sight — laid up carefully in lavender, to be brought out in triumph on some future day.

Henri and his Gabrielle played as usual a conspicuous part in the proceedings of the day. And there was revived on this occasion the almost forgotten old tune, " *Où peut-on être mieux qu'au sein de sa famille?* " (Where can one be better than in the midst of one's family ?), that so constantly greeted Louis XVI. after the failure of his attempts to withdraw from the midst of his large family of rebellious subjects.   It was rather a mocking song of welcome for one whose family had just been rejected by the government that received him with such excessive parade and homage.

It would almost seem that the Emperor Francis and his second self, Count Metternich, had purposely delayed their arrival until the Russian emperor, in the name of the allied sovereigns, had finally refused to acknowledge Napoleon II. and the regency of Maria Louisa.   Yet it is recorded that both emperor and minister were annoyed that the settlement of so weighty a question had taken place in their absence — the grand ceremony of their entry by no means compensating for the disappointment. But "everything," Count Metternich said, "was thoughtlessly accepted in Paris, as if nothing in the world was serious."

Maria Louisa (now with marked affectation always spoken of as the archduchess), perplexed and irresolute, had left Blois with her son for a few days' sojourn at the Petit Trianon. Thence she repaired to Rambouillet, where she waited her husband's departure and her father's arrival, in order to set out on her return to Vienna. The Emperor Alexander visited her at Rambouillet, as he visited Joséphine at La Malmaison, and the ex-Queen Hortense (now Madame Louis Bonaparte) in Paris. It was the general opinion that he ought not to have paid any of those visits, and that he should have especially refrained from presenting himself at La Malmaison. But Joséphine, with characteristic thoughtlessness, was as anxious as others to see the amiable sovereign of the Cossacks and Bashkirs, who had taken Paris and the Parisians under his protection, and was reported to her as more generous, more courteous, and more polite than were the descendants of Saint Louis.

To admire Alexander had become a fashion with the ladies. They spoke of him with rapture, and Joséphine's tribute of admiration was no less enthusiastic than the rest. It was perhaps not wholly disinterested. She was anxious to obtain from the omnipotent czar some definite promise respecting her title of empress, which she was unwilling to exchange for that of Duchesse de Navarre, as had been suggested to her. She had also a vague idea of accompanying Napoleon to Elba, as Maria Louisa was not permitted to do so, had she even been disposed. According to Madame Junot, it was Madame de Rémusat who encouraged Joséphine to carry out this idea. It may, however, be considered certain that such an arrangement, had it been attempted, would have been strongly objected to by Napoleon, and no less so by his mother and sister, who, with more propriety, were about to become companions of his exile.

All the Bonaparte family had left or were leaving France. The Princesse Pauline was in Provence. Madame Lætitia and her brother, Cardinal Fesch, were to set out for Rome on the 17th. Jérôme and Joseph had gone no one knew whither, but with the intention of proceeding, when opportunity offered, to America. Caroline Bonaparte still wore her crown and reigned at Naples. Only at her instance, it was firmly believed, had the intrepid, dauntless Murat, who often quailed before his imperious wife, consented to turn against Napoleon and join the coalition. Lucien was in England. Louis XVIII., judging Lucien's fraternal sentiments by his own, apparently, is said to have suggested to Lucien that he should return to France with him. But Lucien replied that, while his brother was an exile, he would never set foot on the soil of France.

On the 21st, the day after Napoleon's departure, the Duc de Berry arrived. He had a long harangue prepared for the edification of the authorities who went to the barrier of Clichy to receive him. Again he exhibited strong emotional feeling, and renewed his assurances that he and his family returned to France forgetting the wrongs of the past. But, except to the royalists, the Duc de Berry was not exactly the Henri IV. the Parisians expected. He was a pygmy in stature, with a rather large head, which, from the shortness of his neck, seemed driven down between his shoulders. His temper was haughty and irascible, his voice harsh, and his movements were brusque, denoting an angry and impetuous spirit. When in a placid mood his countenance was not unpleasing. His eyes were fine, and his smile pleasant, displaying a good set of teeth. He was thirty-six years of age, and, as far as his more limited resources permitted, had followed a career of dissipation similar to that which had made the heyday of his father's youth so notorious.

The last to appear, heralding the arrival of the Comte de Provence, now fully recognised as Louis XVIII., King of France, was the saintly Duc d'Angoulême. His extreme obesity, his unwieldy movements, and that swaying of the body peculiar

to this branch of the Bourbons — as though the
feet and ankles supported the ponderous mass
with difficulty — were as remarkable in him as in
his uncles, Louis XVI. and Louis XVIII., the
fattest of the fat dauphin's fat family.   Notwithstanding his saintly reputation, his *entourage* of
Jesuit priests, his prayers and masses, the Duc
d'Angoulême was of a violent and arrogant temper.
He was under the delusion that he was a very
great soldier, possessed of a military genius surpassing Napoleon's, but wanting opportunity for
its development.   However, with his enormous
bulk and rosy fat face, he had less of the martial
air and bearing of a soldier than the comfortable
appearance of a well-fed abbot, or prior, of the old
régime — one of those sleek, sleepy, and pious
priests, fonder of the pleasures of the table than
of fasting, penance, and prayer.

CHAPTER VI.

THE restoration of Louis XVIII. may be said to have been inaugurated in London, where he arrived from Hartwell on the 20th of April, at Grillon's Hotel in Albemarle Street, which had been engaged for his temporary residence. On the morrow he made a sort of public triumphal promenade through the streets and parks of the West End. The king, the Princes de Condé, the Ducs de Havre, Duras, Gramont, and Lorges; the king's two favourites, the Comte de Blacas-d'Aulps and le Père Élisée, with other members of his household, occupied seven of the prince regent's state carriages, each drawn by six horses. The servants wore their state liveries; several hundred gentlemen on horseback preceded the king's carriage; and a detachment of cavalry escorted the whole, making up a very pretty show.

Of course there was no lack of spectators —
rails, walls, windows, and pavement, having each
its full complement.   Some French writers say
that the people took the horses from the king's
carriage and, with vociferous hurrahs, drew him
in triumph to his hotel.   But — on the authority
of an eye-witness — the people only took off their
hats as the procession passed, and displayed no
enthusiasm whatever for the "right divine " in the
person of Louis XVIII.   Why indeed should they?
His appearance was not likely to inspire any, and
they knew naught of the intrigues of the regent
and the government in his favour.

On the 22d "the first gentleman in Europe" —
then growing bulky and gouty like his brother of
France — visited the reinstated monarch at his
hotel.   Many of the nobility also paid their respects
to him.   A few hours later the royal visit was
returned.   Louis then bade a final adieu to the
prince regent.   He was effusive in his thanks for
the great service he had done him in urging on
Lord Castlereagh, so early as the beginning of the
campaign : "No compromise, no treaty with Bonaparte.   Support the recall of the Bourbons."   He
believed that for his return to France he was
chiefly indebted to the good offices of the English
prince.

At nine the following morning, with the
Duchesse d'Angoulême and his suite, he left
London, accompanied also by a numerous party

of emigrants. British men-of-war conveyed them to Calais, where, on the 24th, the king and the duchess landed, amidst the enthusiasm (as a French writer says) of the emigrants they had brought back with them.

Louis and his retinue travelled by very easy stages, though the roads, unlike those he had known under the old *régime*, were good, and ample means were at his command for getting on quickly. On the 28th he arrived at the Château de Compiègne. Its imperial splendour and the extensive alterations must have been a great surprise to him, though, as the work of "the usurper," these renovations are said to have caused both him and the duchess no slight indignation. The latter, on taking possession of the boudoir — draped with the finest cashmere shawls, the furniture being similarly covered — crossed herself devoutly when her eye fell on the imperial cipher and crown. At Compiègne, however, the king would have halted for a while. *He* found the new arrangements very comfortable, and he wished to ascertain, before advancing further, whether the political soil of France was yet sufficiently firm to bear him.

For the Liberal party loudly denounced the Peace of Paris, by which the lieutenant-general had signed away on the 23d all the conquests of the republic (Savoy excepted), and those of the empire, and had also given up to the allies the

vast stores and material of war (valued at many
millions) collected by Napoleon, and contained in
the numerous fortresses and arsenals lost to
France by the treaty. The odium of this wholesale signing away of all the territory conquered by
the French arms during the previous twenty-five
years was to be borne by the lieutenant-general,
he being then so popular.

The *salons* of old ladies of the Faubourg St.
Germain resounded with his praises. In no other
country, probably under any circumstances, much
less under the serious political aspect of things
then prevailing in France, would the admiration of
a set of old women for the gay libertine of their
youthful days — whose conquests, however, were
more numerous in the *coulisses* of the theatres and
at opera balls than in the *salons*, which he frequented but rarely —have availed him anything in
smoothing away the difficulties of his position.
But the Comte d'Artois knew that these elderly
dowagers were a power in the state; and to secure
the popularity then needed he had even condescended to whisper pretty flattering speeches to
faded *belles* of the *vilaine noblesse.*

In France there were, and doubtless still are, as
many political intriguers of the "gentler sex" as
of the sterner one. The former are often more
subtle as well as more insinuating than the latter,
and it is the elder women who, in this respect,
generally possess the most real influence. Napo-

leon often made use of wily woman's wit to carry
out his projects. And how much less of evil or
good (whichever it may be considered) would
Prince Talleyrand have effected, deprived of his
devoted band of *belles amies!* Even the *bêtises*
of Madame la Princesse de Benevento — not so
bête perhaps as some people thought her — he at
times was known to have turned to very good
account. "But for the women," Louis XVIII. is
reported to have said, "the Restoration would
have been a bond of peace and universal concord."
Certainly none strove more to make it otherwise
than the morosely pious Duchesse d'Angoulême.

But to return to Compiègne. Thither the great
military grandees, the grand marshals and generals
of the empire, hastened to do homage to their
new sovereign. It was not their fault if they were
not the first of his faithful subjects to welcome
him to his kingdom. But the legislative body had
been on the alert for the earliest news of his
majesty's landing, and had immediately despatched
a deputation to greet him, thus stealing a march
on the marshals, who reached the château some
three or four hours later. They, however, were
not the last to appear, and certainly not the least
enthusiastic in their welcome.

A flattering, fulsome harangue was spoken by
Maréchal Berthier, Prince of Neufchâtel, in the
name of the marshals and officers generally. This
was indeed a deplorable spectacle. All sense of

honour, all self-respect, had apparently become
extinct in the breasts of these men. Their
royalism of a few days' date was vociferously
expressed — the impetuous Maréchal Ney, of all
others, "the bravest of the brave," being the most
eager in giving the signal for the frequent cry of
"*Vive le roi!*" when the king replied to their
address.

And a very ludicrous reply it was. Affecting
to be inspired by the enthusiasm of these renegade
marshals, so far as to ignore the patent fact that
his enormous obesity, his everlasting gout, and a
complication of other maladies, disqualified him
from walking without assistance even so much as
a dozen paces, he exclaimed, half rising from his
seat by his attendant's aid, and as though his soul
were all aflame with military ardour : "Gentlemen,
I trust that France will have no further need of
your swords; but should we be forced again to
unsheath them, I, all gouty as I am, promise to
march with you!" This noble speech, which
might well have provoked a peal of derisive
laughter, elicited warm and prolonged applause.
The marshals and generals in their brilliant imperial uniforms, and decked out with their crosses
and grand cordons of the Legion of Honour, glittering with diamonds, rubies, and emeralds, then
withdrew from the presence of the royal warrior
chief, who in case of need was to succeed the
great captain to whom they owed the decorations,

of which they were unworthy, and even their
martial glory.

"I was rather afraid of those marshals," said
the king to M. Blacas, when the military deputation withdrew; "for I thought to find them ferocious. But they are perfectly tame, and have
neither nails nor teeth. With Bonaparte they
were no doubt to be feared; without him they are
but a puff of smoke — mere playthings in fact."

The provisional government having elaborated
its new constitution, presented it on the 8th of
April to the Comte d'Artois. He had signed the
Treaty of Paris, apparently — and only apparently
— without the sanction of the king; for the terms
of this treaty were the sole conditions on which
he and his family were permitted by the allies to
return to France. He, however, refused to commit his brother to the acceptance of a constitution
based on principles of liberalism so repugnant to
both. When it was laid before Louis XVIII., he
very cavalierly rejected it altogether. He would
have no constitution thrust upon him by his subjects, but he would graciously condescend to grant
them one. This rebuff cooled the royalistic ardour
of the Senate, who refrained from sending a deputation to lay its members collectively at the feet of
the sovereign. But, if not represented as a body,
many of its number separately made the journey
to congratulate the king on his arrival, as did also
a considerable number of the royalist gentry.

M. Blacas, the king's intimate friend, counsellor, and favourite, had given close attention to the fulsome harangues and humble attitude assumed by the new converts to royalism.   The eagerness with which they thronged to Compiègne to do homage and to swear allegiance to the restored dynasty, led him, perhaps rather hastily, to a firm conviction that the reëstablishment of the absolute monarchy of former days was an affair of no difficulty whatever. "His majesty need not trouble himself about reforms and concessions.   But, above all, let him not be hampered, on taking up the reins of power, by any conditions."

Louis, though less confident than his counsellor, yet was in no hurry to inform his zealous but anxiously expectant lieges in what manner he proposed to govern them.   It was in his nature to temporise, to manœuvre.   Yet he was so ill-advised — considering himself of more ancient and lofty lineage than any other European sovereign — as to receive the Emperor Alexander at Compiègne with a sort of haughty condescension, very wounding to the susceptibilities of the all-powerful and popular czar.   Perhaps this was the more noticeable as Louis XVIII. piqued himself on the punctilious observance of the forms of politeness.   He, however, regarded the descendant of the Romanoffs as a mere *parvenu* compared with the descendant of Saint-Louis.   And this *parvenu* came to dictate to him.

Singular mission for the despotic ruler of a nation of serfs! Alexander had resolved on seeing the political liberties of the people, who had so warmly received him, consecrated under his auspices. It was his strong sympathy for everything French that had sustained the enthusiasm with which, on his entry, he was greeted, and had given him so much genuine popularity. It was he, not Louis XVIII., who was king — of all Paris, at least.

And "all Paris" still, to a great extent, was accepted as of old in the sense of "all France." When, therefore, he perceived the supercilious indifference of Louis when pressed on the question of promptly issuing a liberal programme of government to meet the anxious wishes of his people, he made him clearly understand that the gates of the capital would be closed against him if he refused to satisfy the expectations of the constitutional party.

The Russian emperor returned to Paris. The King of France moved on to St. Ouen. There for two days the unyielding M. Blacas strove to fortify the king in a determination to govern according to his own good pleasure; to submit to no dictation; and, in a word, to convince refractory France that the Restoration must be accepted in all things, in its true sense, and as an accomplished fact, including the Bourbon king's motto, "*L'état, c'est moi.*" He fancied, as other re-

turned emigrants did, that France was so delighted to have them all back again that the
people would be only too happy unconditionally
to surrender everything to them.

The realisation of his favourite's arbitrary views
would doubtless have been very agreeable to
Louis XVIII.   But he was too shrewd and clear-
sighted to entertain a hope that a consummation
so devoutly to be wished was possible then, whatever the womb of time might eventually bring
forth.

Yet he still held out, being secretly encouraged
by M. de Talleyrand, who, however, feigned opposition to his views, and agreement with Alexander's. Two days had elapsed, and no proclamation
was forthcoming, the various factions into which
society and the political world were divided interpreting this silence according to their several
hopes and fears. The most powerful of the allies
again interposed. He declared that, the concessions demanded being withheld, the allied armies
could not evacuate France. From thirty thousand
to forty thousand troops must remain there, so
great was the agitation that prevailed throughout
the country.

The king's hand thus forced, the draft of a
manifesto, promising even more liberal and extensive reforms than those of the constitution he had
rejected, was sent to Alexander. Communicated
to the Senate, it made a favourable impression.

This manifesto, known as the " Déclaration de St. Ouen," was signed " Louis Stanislas Xavier, roi de France et de Navarre." Meeting with the approval of the Russian emperor as well as of the Senate, it was intimated to Louis XVIII. that he might now enter Paris.

No time was lost by the king in availing himself of this permission. He was annoyed, indeed, that any conditions had been attached to his entry, as well as at the little anxiety the people had evinced for his presence among them. A spark of jealousy also fired his ample breast when the conviction was forced on him that his despotic ally had more real power in France than he. " It is high time," he said, " that we should show ourselves." The scale must be turned. For — oh, crowning vexation ! — the pious lieutenant-general, the hope of the ultramontanes and ultra-royalists, was courting and obtaining popularity. Slight, active, and still upright in figure, — such a contrast to the elephantine proportions of the august Louis, — daily he might be seen caracoling and displaying his horsemanship before the admiring eyes of the ladies, with all the airs and graces of the Comte d'Artois grown young again. The duchess, too, was much alarmed at this.

But, worse still perhaps, he was scattering with a too lavish hand Napoleon's sixty millions, with which the allies had endowed the king, who never before had had so much cash in reserve. He had

proposed to dole it out in part to the most needy
or importunate of his partisans, reserving, of
course, the lion's share for himself.   Taking all
these untoward circumstances together, it was
time, "high time," as M. Blacas said, echoing his
sovereign's words, "that they should show themselves."

On the morrow, then, the 2d of May, — the
day on which Napoleon arrived at Elba, — Louis
XVIII. entered Paris.

CHAPTER VII.

EITHER the people had grown weary of
welcoming the Bourbons, as severally
they made their appearance in France,
or they were disappointed to find that the divinity
supposed to hedge a king, which they had been
led to believe was conspicuously present in the
person of Louis XVIII., to their eyes was only
conspicuously absent. For it is certain that the
appearance and manners of this "son of Saint
Louis" impressed all who first saw him on the
occasion of his entry far differently from what was
expected by himself and generally hoped for by
his partisans. All was done that the difficult position of affairs permitted to invest the proceedings
of the day with imposing solemnity. It was antici-
pated that this, more readily than festive arrangements, would find its way to the hearts of the
people; would repress any show of ill-feeling;

would awaken respect, and elicit an enthusiastic
reception for the aged prince restored to the
throne of his ancestors after long years of exile.

The city was full of foreign troops. Attended
by them, a grand military *cortège* might have been
effectively arranged. But it was imperative, on
such an occasion, that these alien forces should be
wholly kept out of sight. That the susceptibilities of the monarch and his people might not be
too deeply wounded, French soldiers must escort
him to his capital. But Baron Maubreuil's recruits, "the soldiers of the Restoration," — a set
of ruffians and ragamuffins, — had already disbanded themselves, no attempt having been made
to restrain them.

The temper of the French army — still calling
itself imperial — made insubordination and opposition to the restored dynasty the rule in the
ranks. This ill-feeling was further embittered
by the sight of the white flag audaciously flaunting over the Vendôme column, where so lately
had stood the statue of their emperor. Yet, in
spite of the distrust they inspired, it was necessary that a sufficiently numerous escort should be
formed of these troops. Some of the more popular of their officers were therefore induced, though
but little disposed for the service assigned them,
to reason with their men, and thus lead them to
yield, if not with ready obedience, at least with
less marked unwillingness, to the order to attend

Louis XVIII.
Photo-etching from an old print.

the king on his entry, and otherwise do duty in the ceremony of the day.

Louis XVIII. entered Paris on a bright, sunny May morning, in an open carriage drawn by six horses. He wore a light blue coat with epaulets and gilt buttons, red velvet gaiters, velvet boots, and a round hat. His hair, or wig, was powdered. The grand cross of the Order of Saint Louis was suspended over his white waistcoat, and a large white cockade decorated the left side of his coat ; it had been pinned there by the august fat hands of the prince regent — a parting token of his friendship on bidding a final adieu to the French king.

As he had been placed in his carriage on quitting St. Ouen, his excessive corpulence and chronic gout obliged him immovably to remain. His countenance wore a frigid, defiant expression, that seemed to contradict De Berry's emotional utterance, " Frenchmen, we return to you, forgetting the wrongs of the past " — unless, indeed, the wrongs of the past signified those that the nation had suffered at the hands of the Bourbons. Those they did forget, but on their return were fully purposed to inflict them anew.

On the king's left hand sat the Duchesse d'Angoulême, the daughter of that unfortunate pair whose weakness and incapacity on the one hand, folly and extreme levity on the other, brought so much evil on France and so sad a fate on themselves.

It was natural, however, that their errors should
now be forgotten, and bitter recollections give
place to sympathy, when the sons and daughters
and aged widows of the victims of the red-handed
chief of the Reign of Terror beheld the daughter
of Louis XVI. and Marie Antoinette returning
amongst them.   But more closely were they in
heart attracted towards her when those standing
nearest her carriage told to the crowd around
them, in subdued and respectful tones, " She
weeps."   And many wept with her.   Tears effaced the derisive laugh that had but just before
played on their features when, in reply to the
anxious questioning of the spectators as to which
was the "new king" — for the old Princes de
Condé, father and son, both solemn and severe,
were also in the royal carriage — a voice in the
crowd loudly blurted out, " *C'est ce gros goutteux !*"
(It is that big gouty fellow!)

As if in contempt for this unkingly looking
king, a startling shout of " *Vive la garde impé-
riale !*" burst forth in response, and was again and
again repeated ; but none cried " Long live the
king ! "

The duchess put down the parasol with which
she had partly concealed her emotion, and cast a
penetrating glance on the people.   It was a glance
of intensest hate!   Had its power been equal to
her will, it would have scattered those presumptu-
ous rebels with the full force of a shower of

mitraille. Louis, for his own advantage, would have had the duchess smile on the crowd, and bow unceasingly — representing an angel of pardon and peace, a mediatress, if need were, between them and the awe-inspiring right divine, of which he was the awfully majestic impersonation. But if the Duchesse d'Angoulême was to play the angel *con amore*, it must be in the spirit of an avenging one. As such she returned to France.

She desired to enter Paris attired in deepest mourning. The king strenuously opposed it. It contrasted too strongly with his own gala-costume of red, blue, and white, and glittering cross of Saint Louis. But, more important still, it was perilously impolitic. Yet in spite of these objections — for she had all the wilfulness of Marie Antoinette — the duchess appeared in a dress which, if not actually mourning, was of such sombre hue and exaggerated plainness that the aristocratic dames of the royalist Faubourg, dressed with much elegance for this occasion, gazed on their princess with dismay. If — and they were elate with the expectation — the old *régime* was to be fully revived in its ancient splendour, surely it was not to be minus the laces and ribands, pearl powder and rouge, silks and jewels, and the thousand and one etceteras that made up the graceful feminine *toilette* of that period. The *vilaine noblesse*, as the baronesses and duchesses of the empire were termed, also looked on the royal lady's costume with much wonder ; but with them wonder was mingled with compassion.   She had resided, they said, so long in Germany and England that it was not surprising she should so entirely have lost a Frenchwoman's natural good taste in dress.

But although the Duchesse d'Angoulême made no converts to her dreary style of dressing, she might, with more geniality of temper and more enlightened views of religion, have exerted a very benign influence on the court and society of that day, which would probably have gone far to avert the final downfall of the elder branch of the Bourbons.

This reception, then, of the Most Christian king by his faithful lieges, "in whose love he had found," as he proclaimed, "the restitution of his rights," could not be considered very enthusiastic. Yet royalist writers have spoken of acclamations that rent the air.   And they may have done so ; but the air was not torn and tattered for the king. They tell, too, of the monarch having graciously, if not gracefully, placed his hand on his heart in acknowledgment of this deafening greeting, — so deafening that "*l'empereur*," it seems, was not distinguishable from "Louis XVIII."   Placing his hand on his heart was confessedly a favourite gesture of his.   "It expressed so much," he said, "without the necessity of uttering a word."

But on the occasion in question it may have been but a sign of recognition addressed to a lady

who, charmingly arrayed in white silk, with white
bonnet, flowing white plume, and a bunch of lilies
reposing on her bosom, was standing in a balcony,
and rather demonstratively waving to and fro
either a small white flag or a handkerchief. The
old king had seen this lady before, and expressed
much interest in her. She was in the summer-
time of life, not numbering more than thirty years,
and if not exactly a beautiful woman, decidedly an
elegant one. She was remarkably *spirituelle* and
lively in temper, and was, besides, one of the greatest *intrigantes* in Paris, keeping on the most
excellent terms with all parties and factions, and
with politicians of every hue, whether of her own
or of the lordly sex. On this lady's last visit to
Hartwell, Louis, on taking leave of her, had said,
" *Au revoir à Paris.*"

When suddenly, then, so fair a vision again
beamed on him, he would, not unnaturally, as he
still piqued himself on his gallantry, make an
effort to find the place where his heart should be
and press his gouty hand upon it. It was an
appropriate sign that indeed might well mystify
the indifferent multitude, but would be fully comprehended by the wily Comtesse du Cayla, whose
influence over the king was to prevail to so great
an extent during the next ten years in the secret
councils of state. The unexpected appearance of
his fascinating and talented *amie intime* may have
been to him as the sudden bursting forth of the

sun on a misty morn.   For neither he nor those
who were with him could well fail to perceive the
decidedly hostile attitude assumed by the military
on that day, or to feel, at the least, much chagrined
by it.

That, in the main, stanch, if at times slightly
wavering, royalist, M. de Châteaubriand, rather
naïvely relates * that, dreading the effect which
the personal appearance of Louis XVIII. would
have on the Parisians, he undertook to prepare,
as it were, the way for his entry.   That is, he
wrote an account which was published in the
National, describing the king's arrival at Compiègne, whither with other royalist gentlemen he
went to do homage to his new sovereign.   " Aided
by the Muses," he says, " I idealised the son of
Saint Louis, as it was my aim to make him
known to the Parisians."

As the king approached, he tells them, a confused clamour of " *Vive le roi !* " arose in the air,
with subdued expressions of joy and tenderness.
The blue coat and " simple decorations " are then
described, with the " ample red velvet gaiters
bordered with a small gold cord."   " Seated in
his armchair," continues the chevalier, " wearing
his old-fashioned gaiters, and holding his cane
between his knees, one might have fancied that
he beheld Louis XIV. at the age of fifty."

This was an idealised portrait indeed, and one

* *Mémoires d'outre-tombe.*

that did much injustice to the magnificent *Grand Monarque*. He, at the age of fifty, was still a man of noble presence, tall, erect, and robust. He would have disdained velvet gaiters and velvet boots ; for he was a great walker, too, then and for many years after. Louis XVIII., on the contrary, could not walk two yards without assistance. He was also within a few months of his sixtieth year, and in constitution old before his time — the victim of gluttony, disgusting to behold.

This interesting object, according to Châteaubriand's account, " returning from exile, destitute of everything, without a suite, without guards, without wealth, has nothing to give, almost nothing to promise. He alights from his carriage ; he leans on the arm of a young woman ; he shows himself to the captains, who have not yet seen him ; to the grenadiers, who scarcely knew his name. ' Who is this man ?' they ask. ' It is the king,' is the reply ; and all present fall at his feet."

Commenting on his own statement, the chevalier continues : " What I said of these warriors, in order to attain the object I had in view, was true as regarded the principal officers. But I lied (*je mentais*) as far as the men were concerned." That he lied to no purpose is seen by what follows.

" There rises up vividly before me," he says,

" the spectacle of which I was an eye-witness when Louis XVIII. entered Paris on his way to Notre-Dame.   He was spared the humiliating sight of the foreign troops — some regiments of the old guard lining the road from the Pont Neuf to Notre-Dame.   But I do not think that human countenances ever before expressed anything so terrible, so menacing.   These bronzed and scarred soldiers, the conquerors of Europe, deprived of their leader, were compelled to salute in the invaded capital of Napoleon, and under the surveillance of the hidden army of Russians, Prussians, etc., an old king — an invalid, not of the battle-field, but of age and infirmity.

" Some of them, by a movement of the head, lowered the fronts of their tall hair caps over their eyes, as if to hide from their view what was passing before them.   Rage or contempt was strongly expressed on the contracted features of others, while their closely set teeth, gleaming through their moustaches, gave them the expression of tigers ready to spring on their prey.   It must, however, be conceded that it was trying these men greatly to select them for such a service.   No doubt it was to many of them as the suffering of martyrdom, and it was well they were not then called on to exact vengeance.

" At the end of the line of troops a young officer of hussars sat on his horse with his sword drawn.   Rage was in his face, and he was pale as death. As he glared on the scene with the suppressed fury of a savage, his horse, yielding to the pressure of the rider's spur, slightly advanced. The king was then passing, and the temptation to seize that moment to rush upon and attack him was, apparently, with difficulty resisted."

It is evident from the above that the entry of Louis XVIII. into Paris was no triumphal one. The reception he met with, from all but the emigrant party he brought back with. him, was rather a protest against the conduct of the allies in thrusting on the nation a ruler abhorrent to it, a man in whom no interest was felt, and who had not the qualities to inspire any ; a member of a hated dynasty already expelled, and justly, too, for its oppressive and despotic rule.

CHAPTER VIII.

HE month of May, 1814, was a very gay month in the capital of France; in spite, too, of the special grievances of the Bonapartists, constitutionalists, republicans, and revolutionists — all more or less indisposed towards the royalist restoration. Yet all seemed willing to enjoy the brief honeymoon of festivity and pleasure, though it boded neither concord nor happiness in the future; for the governed and governing parties, distrusting each other, were secretly marshalling their forces, — notwithstanding the promised charter, — on the one hand to oppose and resist, on the other to crush and subdue.

As soon as Louis XVIII. and his family were installed in the luxuriously furnished Palace of the Tuileries, a fresh foreign invasion of Paris took place. Visitors flocked in in overwhelming numbers. The English, most numerous of all, were among the first to make their appearance. To the greater part a visit to Paris was a new sensation; while the few who had spent a short time there during the peace of 1802 were amazed at the change which the imperial capital had since undergone. The improvements — which an almost continual state of preparation for war would seem to have left no time for — were not only numerous, but good, and the embellishments in excellent taste, transforming Paris into a magnificent city compared with what it was when it came into Napoleon's hands.

The Bourbons and emigrants of '89 and '90 confessed that they scarcely recognised it. But this confession was professedly made in sorrow, as a lament for the squalor that had disappeared. Extreme royalists were known to have fervently expressed their gratitude to heaven for staying the hand of the "Corsican usurper," ere he had realised his sweeping and impious project of erecting a new city on the site of the fever-harbouring capital of the descendants of Saint Louis.

But the king, it appears, was perfectly content both with the comfort and splendour of the quarters which his Corsican predecessor had vacated for him. His thorough appreciation of the luxurious ease they afforded him added considerably to his enjoyment on finding himself, after so many

ups and downs, so many alternations of hope and
fear, firmly seated on the throne of France. With
extraordinary tenacity he clung to that throne and
to the possession of the long-coveted privileges of
royalty, — to such a degree that, although but a
mass of disease and infirmities, with one foot well
in the grave and the other ready to follow, he for
ten years lived on, sustained during the last five
almost by the force of his will alone, in a state of
physical decay that almost precluded the hope of
a life of as many months' duration.

The Comte d'Artois and the Duc and Duchesse
d'Angoulême were also sumptuously lodged at the
Tuileries, in the Pavillon Marsan. But the un-
amiable duchess, as if to mark her supreme contempt for the splendour surrounding her, had the
folly to order the attendants to search the apartments for an old spinet, left in the palace when
the mob invaded it in 1792. It was to be brought
to her boudoir, and an elegant instrument, formerly belonging to Joséphine, was to give place
to it. But, alas! the spinet could not be found.
It did not seem to occur to the duchess that the
mob who wantonly destroyed so much that was
really valuable would not have been likely to
spare the spinet if it fell in their way; and she
was no less unmindful of many subsequent scenes
of riot and confusion that took place at the Tuileries before it was repaired and refurnished for
the imperial court. Evidently, she fancied that

the sacrilegious hand of the usurper had been laid on the royal spinet. Probably it had served to light the fires of some of the *sans-culottes*, or had helped to heap up a bonfire round which, waving their caps of Liberty, they had danced the Carmagnole.

But to return to the foreign visitors, of whom every unwieldy diligence, every swift (swift for those days) *malle-poste*, every ponderous family travelling-carriage, brought its contingent. There were, indeed, unusual attractions for strangers in Paris at that particular juncture, the chief of them being that the greater part of the royalty of Europe was assembled within its walls, and to be seen, one may say, at a single glance.

There were the four great Christian potentates of Russia, Austria, Prussia, and France; for Louis XVIII. must be accepted as one of them, though many regarded him in the light of a mere *pis-aller,* a makeshift, stopping a gap until a more eligible chief was forthcoming. Then there were the minor kings and sovereign princes — creations, for the most part, of the magic wand of Napoleon; also the most distinguished military chiefs, the greatest of all excepted, as well as two of his former aides-de-camp, men of lowly birth, but of high military renown, who had developed into royal personages, and were now leagued with the enemies of their great commander. They were the unfortunate Joachim Murat, King of Naples, and the very fortunate Charles Jean Bernadotte, then crown prince, and afterwards king, of Sweden.

Besides these, there were those important personages, the ambassadors of all nations, whose duty it was to give *fêtes* to the monarchs, the princes, and distinguished visitors. Generally, too, there was an ambassadress to do the honours of the *salon*. Otherwise it would have fallen almost wholly on those wealthy turncoats, the great dignitaries and military grandees of the empire, to entertain monarchical Paris. The old nobility of the Faubourg St. Germain, whether then resident in, or only returning to, France, declared themselves too poor to receive. They had also the valid excuse of having to afford a home and substantially provide table to several uninvited guests of the allied army. The necessity of giving up their best rooms as quarters to foreign officers was a great grievance to many of the old French families. Yet the return of a Bourbon king, and the proposed revival of the good old times, should have amply compensated them for this temporary inconvenience.

Louis had condescended to announce that, early in June, probably, it would be his *bon plaisir* to confer on his faithful lieges the promised new constitution. *En attendant*, King Solomon still reigned, and all the municipal authorities were Russian or German. In one or other of those languages proclamations for the edification of the

Parisians constantly decorated the walls of Paris. And very diligently, if ineffectually, did the people puzzle their brains to make out what such outlandish gibberish could mean.

Ludicrous scenes often occurred at the passport office between the foreign officials and travellers arriving or departing. The former gentlemen, — or, if you please, jacks in office, — when French or English was spoken, would shake their heads most deprecatingly. When by rare chance a traveller appeared who was able to speak a few words of either of the tongues then in vogue in Paris, it was pathetic to behold how imploringly his aid was sought by his distracted and less accomplished countrymen. In short, where, as in the case of passports, it was necessary at that time to be especially clear and explicit, confusion worse confounded reigned.

The English were generally reproached with making everything dear, when they might with more reason have complained that everything was made dear for them. The charges at hotels and for private apartments were raised at least cent. per cent. The restaurateur's prices rapidly rose in the same ratio, and every other tradesman, whether he supplied necessaries or luxuries, adopted a similar tariff. Naturally all were bent on making hay while the sun shone. There was also a real and increasing difficulty in fully supplying the wants of this influx of foreign guests,

Daily they continued to stream in, and new hotels and boarding-houses were needed for their accommodation. Speedily, too, they were established, in more or less expensive style, to suit all tastes and purses, from the wealthy and extravagant to the less amply provided and frugal. It was then that *Galignani's Messenger* was first issued for the especial benefit of English visitors.

Not many persons outside of France at that time possessed any competent knowledge of the French language. But as the English were great frequenters of the theatres, — content, apparently, to see the acting, while understanding little of what was said, — a mirthful piece, " *Les Anglais pour rire,*" was produced for their enlightenment, being a sort of mirror (a slightly distorting one, certainly), held up by the French to their English visitors, to enable them to see how British eccentricities of costume and manners impressed the Parisian mind.

English ladies, however, could not be reproached with unwillingness to adopt French fashions. Their difficulty at this early stage of the transitional period was to know what French fashions were, or were likely to be. It was of course assumed that they were to obliterate those of the empire. There were whisperings in the air that, so far as the court of the Tuileries was concerned, fashion, like everything else, was to take a backward leap of a quarter of a century, and all was to be restored as existing in the early months of '89. This seemed to predicate a revival of paniers and plumes, powder, patches, and paint. Should it really prove so, a hope was expressed that it would be minus the fashionable vices that prevailed in the dissolute court of Versailles at the period when those accessories of the *toilette*, and even the vices, were *de rigueur*.

While awaiting the fiat of the duchess in this important matter, many English *miladis* as well as *milors* (for on all who had cash in abundance and liberally disbursed it that Anglo-French title was conferred) were roaming about Paris, and especially exploring its most obscure nooks and corners, in search of rare specimens of old cabinet work, escritoires, *guéridons*, etc. Old lace, ivories, china, pictures, and rare or choicely bound books, were often picked up for small sums, and were as eagerly purchased for large ones. Anything, in fact, of an artistic character found a ready sale on the assurance that it had been obtained — heaven only knew how (for these enthusiasts, of course, asked few questions) — from one of the ransacked palaces or hôtels of the old nobility.

Some amateurs of *bric-à-brac* were very successful in their quest. Others, having merely the love of collecting, without any special knowledge to guide them as to the real value of their purchases, made very bad bargains. Dealers in those things were quick to discern on whom they could or could not palm off inferior or sham *objets d'art* as specimens of the tasteful style and patient workmanship of the olden time.

But if hunting up old curiosity shops was the occupation of the few, pleasure was the business of the many.   The king's announced intention of being present at the Grand Opéra to hear Sacchini's " *Œdipe à Colone*," and that the duchess and other members of his family would accompany him, caused an overwhelming demand for places.   Not many cared for the opera ; but to secure a few inches of standing-room where, without being crushed to death, a glimpse could be obtained of the restored Bourbon family, large sums were in many instances paid.

The crush was the greater because it was known that the opportunities of seeing the king in public would be rare ; while the duchess's disapproval of theatrical entertainments, her aversion to all *fêtes* except those of the Church, all pomp and parade unless in connection with ecclesiastical ceremonies and priestly processions, had already got noised about.   As neither all foreign visitors nor all Parisians could be received at court, they were therefore the more anxious to avail themselves of perhaps the solitary chance now afforded them of gazing on royalty.

It was no easy matter for the king's personal attendants to get his majesty comfortably seated in the royal, so lately imperial, box, even with the aid of the mechanical chair by which he was raised or lowered to get in or out of his carriage. There would scarcely have been more difficulty in placing him in full marching order at the head of an army, had he been called upon to fulfil the promise so valiantly made to the marshals. The duchess at first declined to attend; she regarded any festive arrangements as sacrilegious while the expiatory ceremonies in connection with the death of Louis XVI. and his queen were unfulfilled. But the king decreed otherwise, and the duchess, with very ill grace, yielded to his will.

By her order no diamonds were to be worn; to spare, it was said, the returned emigrant ladies of the old nobility, who had few probably, and in some instances none, of those dazzling gems, the mortification of being outshone by the ostentatious display she imagined the *vilaine noblesse* would make, unless thus restrained. Her own dress was of rigid simplicity. But even she could perceive that both good taste and elegance were conspicuous in the *toilettes* of the ladies she affected to disdain, and would have banished from her court, had not Louis XVIII. been far too astute to permit it. He even proposed, in a modified sense, to continue Napoleon's system of fusion.

The king's mind was therefore made up to be condescendingly gracious to the new nobility, and to bestow his inane, insincere smiles on the generals' wives, also on those of the officers of the imperial household whose husbands had been most obsequious, and most prompt in giving in their adhesion to the monarchy. The Bourbons were said to have owed their restoration much more to the women of the empire than to the men. But when the feminine part of the old and new order of things were brought into contact — their position at court being reversed — the *grandes dames* of the empire declined to take the second place, while the ladies of the old *régime* as resolutely refused to cede the *pas* to those new-fangled duchesses and princesses. Eventually the clash of wounded female pride and undue lofty pretensions proved almost as fatal as the clash of arms to Louis's cosy enjoyment of the pleasures and privileges of his newly acquired regal honours.

But for the present those antagonistic feelings lay dormant. Curiosity was the prevailing sentiment in the brilliant audience anxiously awaiting the appearance of the royal party. Ladies were present in far greater number than on the occasion of the Russian emperor's first visit to the Opéra. With rare exceptions, all were attired in white silk or white muslin. A few white feathers appeared — a timid venture on the part of those who were not yet aware that, in spite of her austerity, the duchess, who had inherited her mother's fondness for nodding plumes, sometimes yielded to the weakness of wearing them. Pearls, not being forbidden, were profusely worn by their fortunate possessors, those of the Duchesse d'Abrantès being remarkable for their size and purity. Of course there was no stint of white lilies. It was early in the season for them in the immediate neighbourhood of Paris; but they were procured from the South regardless of cost or trouble. Mixed with white lilac they formed a charming and .odorous bouquet, and, as almost every lady carried one, the result of the white dresses and natural white flowers was a general diffusion of sweetness and light.

But if diamonds and glittering jewels were denied to the ladies, they sparkled and shone in lustrous profusion in stars, crosses, and grand crosses on diplomatic uniforms, and the various military uniforms of foreign officers, who, in rather large number, represented the allied armies. Some English visitors' eyes happened to fall on the new duke (Lord Wellington was first greeted in Paris by this new distinction). He seemed desirous of avoiding recognition, but, his presence being detected, some applause followed. It was mingled, however, with hisses, therefore speedily suppressed. The Parisians, in the mood they were then in, would doubtless have gladly accepted Alexander as their king, had it pleased him to displace the son of Saint Louis; but Wellington and English officers generally were far from being in favour with the people, however well they were received in the *salons*.

But, attention! The royal party enters. The whole house rises. The king, seated in his chair, is wheeled in. Only his head and ample bust are visible to the audience. But his face is so florid, and he smiles so benignantly right and left — as it were the sun shining on the just and unjust — that some of his good people of Paris are quite taken with him, and the ladies especially admire "*sa belle vieillesse*," as they term his seeming green old age. During the first months of his reign, when he dreamed of being able to do as it pleased him with his own, — that is, to put on the strong curb he had in store to restrain any further disposition to restiveness on the part of his supposed repentant subjects, — Louis was literally, as the old adage says, as happy as a king, and, until a change came o'er the spirit of his dream, when he found that he was curbed himself by his own hated Charter, really seemed destined late in the autumn of life, and in defiance of gout, to enjoy a Saint Martin's summer.

The morose, resentful duchess, however, has smiles for none. A slight and haughty bend of the head is the only notice she deigns to take of the very friendly greeting of the audience. The Comte d'Artois and his sons are less ungracious, the gloomy face of the duchess being therefore more generally remarked. It is evident to all that she will bring the Bourbons no increase of popularity. The sad events of her early years had naturally, as those most friendly towards her suggest, had their influence on her character, and to the seclusion in which she since had lived might be attributed in some measure the great stiffness and frigidity of her manners.

Personally the Duchesse d'Angoulême was not unpleasing, but her nature was so utterly unsympathetic that she repelled rather than attracted. Few, very few, probably, who were present at the Opéra that evening, besides the king and his family, had ever seen Marie Antoinette, but her portraits were familiar to most persons. Though always greatly flattered, the daughter's likeness to them, if not striking, was at least perceptible. The grace, which was really the chief charm of the heedless, unfortunate queen, was however wanting in her daughter, while the haughty air and vindictive temper which characterised Marie Antoinette were inherited to the full.

The duchess could not be reproached with the same lamentable levity of conduct that brought on the queen and others such heavy misfortune ; she erred in the opposite extreme, and should have wholly adopted the religious life, or, on returning to France, have abstained from interfering in affairs of state. She had great influence over the weak mind of the reformed *roué*, her father-in-law. But her influence was most baneful; for she had neither judgment nor toleration. Adversity had taught her nothing, and she was guided only by a spirit of vengeance.

Like her mother, she was unfortunate in her husband. It was proposed to marry her to the Archduke Charles, after her liberation from the Temple in exchange for French prisoners in Austria. Her own inclination, it appears, favoured this proposal; but Louis XVIII., then Comte de Provence (who at her baptism had endeavoured to fix on her the stigma of illegitimacy), stepped in and opposed it, and insisted on her marrying the Duc d'Angoulême. Having no heirs himself, he was so generous as to desire that the crown of France should not escape her in the event of his restoration. But, unhappily, both crown and happiness escaped her by her marriage with Angoulême. There was much to excite sympathy in the history of the daughter of Louis XVI. But she rejected it, and persistently repulsed all who were kindly disposed towards her.

It is not, then, to be wondered at that she gazed with stoical indifference on the gay scenes at the Opera-house. Indeed, it may be asserted, not only of her, but generally, as regarded the music, that a more inattentive audience perhaps never before assembled within its walls. To most persons the centre of attraction was not the stage, but the party occupying the royal boxes, royalty in its turn (save and except the duchess, who sat silent, gloomy, and *distraite*) being chiefly intent on keenly, if furtively, scrutinising the audience.

The orchestra exerted itself with little success to attract unlistening ears, and the best efforts of the singers to awaken attention were as scantily rewarded. But at last the opera came to an end, and the king, who, it was suspected, was dozing, was being wheeled off, as the house rose, and a few shouts of "*Vive le roi!*" were heard. This roused him, and a movement of his chair bringing him face to face with the audience, he graciously bent his head and smiled his approbation.

His party followed him, and many of the audience also beat a hasty retreat. But there was a ballet to follow, and it seemed likely to receive more attention than the opera, the great attraction of the evening being withdrawn.

It was noticed that the Duc de Berry had returned, but that he kept well back in his box. It was whispered about, too, that he waited the end of the ballet to escort two or three *belles danseuses* to La Bagatelle, where he supped with his friends after the theatre or opera. La Bagatelle was the celebrated *petite maison* belonging to the Comte d'Artois, who spent on its decoration two millions which his brother Louis XVI. gave him out of the impoverished treasury for the purpose of paying his debts. Already it was partly restored, not only in its former splendour, but to its former uses.   The pious count had presented it to the Duc de Berry at the latter's request, and the orgies for which it was notorious in his father's gay youth were being resumed in all their former shamelessness.

CHAPTER IX.

Grand Marshals of the Empire. — The "Bravest of the Brave" in Tears. — *Salon* of the Duchesse d'Abrantès. — The Governor of Paris. — An Extravagant Pair. — Death of Général Junot. — Royal Promises. — The Right of the *Tabouret*. — Living on Vain Hopes. — The *Polonaise*. — A Faithless Friend. — Royal Condescension. — Death of Joséphine.

ERHAPS nowhere in Paris during this brief festive period were the enemies of Napoleon more courteously welcomed or splendidly entertained than at the sumptuous hôtels of the Prince de Moskowa,* the Duc de Ragusa,† and Madame Junot, Duchesse d'Abrantès. The titles and princely estates heaped on them by Napoleon, their share of the immense spoils of war, and generally their richly dowered wives, had placed the grand marshals among the wealthiest men of the empire.

Maréchal Ney was the first to offer a grand *déjeûner* to the Emperor Alexander, and to follow it up by a splendid *fête* in his honour. Within the short space of a month, this brave soldier, so singularly impetuous and impressionable, had pleaded the cause of his chief before the now all-powerful czar, had urged the claims of the King

---

* Maréchal Ney.   † Maréchal Marmont.

of Rome, and the establishment of the regency.
A few days later he was on his way to Compiègne
with other turncoat marshals (if turncoats they
were) to greet the new master, whom they welcomed in a fulsome harangue.   He now entertains
the emperor of all the Russias, who with courteous speeches repays his hospitality.   And this
"goodness and graciousness" on the part of the
hero of the *fête* so overwhelm the "bravest of
the brave" that, unable to restrain his emotion,
he melts into tears.   Such conduct as Maréchal
Ney's would seem to confirm the opinion held by
many, that at least some of Napoleon's officers
were but feigning to be deserters, under the
impression that the career of their emperor was
not yet ended.

Marmont's treachery was more deliberate, and
was certainly real.   It was remarked that he
always appeared restless and ill at ease.   He was
especially abrupt, too, almost offensively so,
towards the English.   However, Madame la
Duchesse de Ragusa (the banker Perregaux's
daughter) presided in a fine suite of *salons;* receiving visitors of all nations, and doing the honours with the grace and tact that might be
expected in a lady brought up under the vigilant
eye of so perfect a mistress of courtly usages as
the famous Madame Campan.

More attractive still was the *salon* of the young
widow of Général Junot.   The Hetman Platoff and

his people being transferred to other quarters, she
was enabled to receive her numerous guests with
more befitting distinction. They comprised the
élite of the capital, both of the invaded and
invaders. Of the latter, Blücher was the only
general to whom she made exception. Of his
presence she was so intolerant as to leave the
room and refuse to reappear, when, invited by Lord
Cathcart, — who seems to have omitted to men-
tion it to her, — the rough old Prussian soldier
came to dine with the English commander. It
was unfortunate, too, that amongst the diplomatists, Baron Hardenberg alone should have been
distasteful to her. For it was Prussia's good
graces she had then most need of, the hereditary
estates conferred on Général Junot by Napoleon
lying chiefly within the Prussian territory.

Pleasing in person, perfectful graceful and
attractive in manner, well educated, accomplished
and witty, Napoleon, whose keen insight into
character usually enabled him to put the right
persons into the right places, had approved of
Mdlle. Laure de Permon, with whom Général
Junot was then deeply in love, to fill in society the
second place in the empire — that of the wife of
the Governor of Paris. Junot and his young bride
were well fitted for their prominent position; and
the wealth they so suddenly became possessed of
they lavished on all sides for the glorification of
the empire.

Their establishment was almost royal — perhaps one should rather say imperial — in its splendour. The *toilettes* of " Madame la Gouvernante," as Napoleon named her, rivalled in elegance those of the empress ; while M. le Gouverneur, a handsome man and a gay Lothario, though he laughed at the effeminacy of Murat, who spent two million *francs* yearly in feathers, did not disdain an ample quantity of diamonds and gold embroideries for his personal adornment.   The governor's liveries were scarcely distinguishable from the emperor's.   His fine stud of thoroughbred horses surpassed the imperial one.   His stock of choice wines was unrivalled in Paris, and the banquets at which they were served were worthy of them.   The host was genial, the hostess charming, and nightly in her *salons* she provided for her guests an ever-varying round of amusements.   Indeed, strangers visiting Paris were not less anxious to obtain the *entrée* to the *salons* of Madame la Gouvernante, than to be presented at the court of the empress.

To keep up this style of living the governor's appointments were of course immense.   Napoleon was liberal in such matters.   But Général Junot and his wife far exceeded in their expenditure his utmost calculations, and soon were overwhelmingly in debt.   This did not please Napoleon, who, if he liked to dazzle the Parisians with pomp and parade, also liked order and method, impossible though he found it to impress those about him

with the same orderly views. He was compelled
to come to the governor's rescue, and did not
spare him a severe lecture. Madame he blamed
in a more playful manner, and assured her of his
continued friendship by pinching her ears and
pulling her nose.

This sort of life went on for some years, varied
by a command in several campaigns, an embassy,
a viceroyalty, etc. Junot was fanatically devoted
to Napoleon. He was of a good *bourgeois* family,
and educated for the bar ; but his sudden elevation to almost fabulous wealth and great power,
together with the many wounds he received in
battle, chiefly in the head, ultimately affected him
mentally. Towards the end of 1813, while suffering from brain fever at his father's house in Bur-
gundy, whither he had been brought from the
Illyrian provinces, he jumped from a window in
a fit of madness, and was so much injured that
the result was speedy death.

Napoleon's career was then drawing towards its
close, and the royalists were plotting and intriguing
to hasten his downfall. The Duchesse d'Abrantès, though she professes great admiration for Napoleon in her Mémoires, — written in poverty,
when probably she looked back on her days of
grandeur with a sigh of regret, — was no sincere
friend of his. She was suspected of being concerned in the royalist plots, on returning to Paris
in 1814. The Duc de Rovigo (Général Savary),

Minister of Justice, then brought her a message of sympathy from the emperor, with a promise of pensions for herself and children. But at the same time he requested her to leave the capital, and reside for a time at some twenty or thirty leagues distant. She refused, and wrote to Napoleon. The letter was intercepted, and came into the Emperor Alexander's hands. The capitulation soon followed. The duchess reopened her *salons*, and resumed the old style of living, though burdened with debt, and now without any assured income. Very promptly she may be said to have given adhesion to the new order of things, hoping to obtain from Louis XVIII. what she could no longer expect from Napoleon.

She was brilliant in white silk, pearls, and lilies at royalty's first public appearance, and in the same *costume de rigueur* attended the Duchesse d'Angoulême's reception. She pronounced the duchess an angel, without the qualifying adjective most persons used ; she was pleased with Louis's reception of her, for he very graciously promised to grant all she asked, but unfortunately forgot to fulfil his promises. However, he smiled on her with his insipid, deceitful smile, and assumed those mawkish airs of affected gentleness which he fancied made him interesting in ladies' eyes. He spoke of his recollection of her mother as one of the *belles* of society in his younger days, and alluded to her uncle, Prince Demetrius Comnène, as "*des nôtres;*" thus acknowledging the claim of that family (Greek originally) to imperial descent, and placing Madame d'Abrantès far above the rest of the *vilaines duchesses*. It was giving her her tabouret at once; for, amongst other obsolete court usages, the right of the tabouret was to be revived.

Of course she was pleased, but would have been better pleased had she been assured of keeping that magnificent château and wide domain of Raincy, where she and Junot had entertained both royal and imperial guests. It was not to be. Louis Philippe, Duc d'Orléans, claimed it, and it was restored to him, with many more estates than his father, Égalité, had ever possessed. At all events, the Bourbons apparently favoured the Duchesse d'Abrantès, and it seemed not improbable that she was destined again to shine in society as one of its bright, particular stars — perhaps less brilliantly than in the palmy days of the empire, but with soft, subdued refulgence, derived from the divine light of the monarchy.

This being the case, her *salons*, which otherwise would have been thinly attended, were at once thronged by all who desired also to bask in the sunshine of royal favour. In this way her credit was sustained, and her already overwhelming debts greatly increased. Who could doubt, or presume to ask, payment from a lady whose hôtel

was the rendezvous of the most illustrious personages then in Paris — Russian, German, English,
Austrian.

The Emperor Alexander was a frequent visitor.
He sought to interest Frederick William in her
favour, with a view of obtaining his consent to her
son's retention of Junot's estate at Aix-la-Chapelle.
The king was willing to do so, but not unreasona-
bly required that her sons should become Prussian
subjects.   She indignantly rejected his proposal,
and with it of course the estate.   She lived on
vain hopes fostered by Louis's vague promises.
Yet had she been content to live in retirement
with her four young children, the money she obtained by disposing of the treasures contained in
her sumptuous hôtel in the Rue l'Élysée, and part
of her magnificent jewels, would have afforded her
a competency.   But this and other large sums she
received — amongst them 80,000 *francs* for the
restoration of the famous Portuguese Bible which
Junot brought from Lisbon — she soon squandered.

At the magnificent *fête* given during this month
of May by Prince Schwarzenberg to the allied
sovereigns at the Château of St. Cloud, where he
and his staff were installed, the Emperor Alexander introduced the *polonaise*.   It was not very
successful as a dance, but French ladies thought
it delightfully suited for veiling an intrigue, or for
sentimental conversation.   His majesty prome-
naded with the Duchesse d'Abrantès, whose dia-

monds and emeralds drew forth on this occasion as much admiration and envy as her fine Oriental pearls had excited at the Opéra.

But retrenchment at this period Madame d'Abrantès never dreamed of. How should she? Habit had made luxurious surroundings mere ordinary necessaries to her. For some years she had been of almost as much importance in Paris as the empress herself. At Lisbon she and Junot had played king and queen right royally. To sink at once, then, into a private station, a widow of slender means, was impossible to her. Alas! only dire necessity brought her to it. For the present, however, she reigns triumphant, entertaining the *élite* of Europe, and now, as during the empire, a queen of society, a brilliant woman, highly talented, of great musical ability, and a most gracious and perfect hostess.

None was more assiduous in his visits to the hôtel in the Rue l'Élysée, and none was received there more on the footing of friendship, than Prince Metternich, both during the time of his embassy to the imperial court, and during the occupation of Paris by the allied armies.

Yet in the fifth volume of the "Metternich Memoirs," which include the diaries of the prince's third wife, "Clément," as the princess calls her model husband, is referred to as speaking very disparagingly of Madame d'Abrantès, also of Madame Récamier. The princess regrets that

"Clément" has not time to write all he knows and tells so amusingly of these distinguished women, in order, she says, "that posterity might be enlightened respecting them, and be shown the reverse of the medal" which, metaphorically speaking, their compatriots have struck in their honour.

But the Duchesse d'Abrantès was not the only *grande dame* of the imperial *régime* who hastened to seek the favour of Louis XVIII. Even the Empress Joséphine condescended to request an interview, being anxious about the retention of her title, and influenced in some degree by curiosity to see the *"gros goutteux"* who had displaced Napoleon. When ushered into his royal presence, her stately step, her dignified bearing, made so great an impression on him that, momentarily forgetting both his gout and his saintly descent, a sudden impulse prompted him to rise to receive her.

This was, indeed, a most unaccustomed act of courtesy in one who thought all the potentates of Europe greatly his inferiors, and who, waiving all ceremony, invariably took the *pas* of the royal and imperial personages then in Paris, when he did them the honour of inviting them to dine with him.

The ex-Queen Hortense accompanied her mother. Louis was graciously pleased greatly to admire her. She conversed charmingly, he said, and was a model of grace. The Emperor Alexander, who took much interest in her, had already spoken to the king on her behalf, and Louis therefore generously conferred on her the title of Duchesse de Saint-Leu. But it was the title only; the château and domain of that name, which until then she had possessed without the title, were taken from her for restoration to the old Duc de Bourbon-Condé.

Ere a fortnight from this time had passed away, poor Joséphine, so fearful of descending from the rank of empress to that of Duchesse de Navarre, and so distressed at the fate of Napoleon, had breathed her last. A cancerous disease, brought rapidly to a crisis by the great anxieties of her own and her daughter's position, caused her death, on the 29th of May, 1814. It was a great shock to many persons, and to a numerous and attached circle of friends. Both her son and her daughter were with her; for the convention of the 10th of April having put an end to Eugène's viceroyalty, he and his wife passed through Tyrol as fugitives, and reached Munich with difficulty. Thence they journeyed to Paris, arriving in time to have the *triste* consolation of attending their mother's death-bed.

Eugène was well received by Louis XVIII., who, however, had the bad taste to offer him a marshal's *bâton* and a command in his army. He was both surprised and annoyed when his offers were declined. " He spoke of his rank," said the king, " and did not even thank me."

Eugène attended the Congress. His title of prince was confirmed to him. But from that time he withdrew from public affairs, and retired to the principality of Eichstadt in Bavaria. His father-in-law created him Duc de Leuchtenberg and first peer of the kingdom.

CHAPTER X.

HE treaty between Louis XVIII. and
the sovereigns of the coalition was
definitively signed at Paris on the 30th
of May. The Emperors of Russia and Austria,
the King of Prussia, and the sovereign princes of
Germany, almost immediately after took leave of
the king, and left Paris for London, to pay a brief
visit to their ally the prince regent.

Their next destination was Vienna, where preparations were making for holding the Congress.
Already near seven hundred persons had arrived
there, all in some way connected with the various
missions and embassies, or forming part of the
suite of the allies. There was some difficulty, it

appears, suitably to lodge this influx of official
people.   Yet the Viennese hostelries were daily
receiving orders to retain rooms for at least twice
that number of mere visitors, bent only on amusement.   All the world was then travelling, and the
English especially.   For so many years excluded
from the Continent, they were now migrating in
shoals from Paris to the Austrian capital, where
the interests of Europe were about to be discussed,
and where also it was expected that this grave
business of state would be enlivened by a good
deal of festivity and pleasure.   And so it proved.

But "the real object of the Congress of Vienna,"
writes Prince Metternich in his Memoirs, "was
to divide among the conquerors the spoil taken
from the vanquished.   Such grand views as the
reconstruction of social order, regeneration of the
political system, etc., though certainly propounded,
were merely fine phrases, whose purpose, besides
that of satisfying the people, was to impart an air
of greater dignity and grandeur to this solemn
conclave of princes and kings.

At all events, the departure of the allied sovereigns from Paris freed Louis XVIII. from their
tutelage, and from the presence of the czar, of
whose influence in society, and popularity with
the Parisians generally, he was beginning to feel
very jealous.   He has now no rival near his
throne, save a wily intriguer of his own family.
But his schemes, he believes, are more likely to

prove annoying to his successor than to himself ;
though he proposes to keep a vigilant eye on the
Duc d'Orléans and his partisans.   But, at all
events, Louis now feels that he is really King of
France, and by the grace of God in full possession
of his hereditary rights.

His coronation is talked of.   An early date is
proposed ; for life is precarious, to this royal
glutton especially so.   And as gout and other
infirmities render moving about both fatiguing
and difficult to him, the Abbey of Saint-Denis, or
the church of Notre-Dame de Paris, is suggested
as preferable, for so long and wearying a ceremony, to the cathedral of Rheims, notwithstanding
its ancient and holy associations.   But first the
royal Charter — the new constitution which Louis
graciously deigns to confer on the nation — must
be read to the Chamber, then publicly proclaimed
to the people.

For this purpose the Senate — or rather that
part of it only which professes royalist principles
— is convoked for the 4th of June, together with
the legislative body.   Some portion of the old
ceremonial of the monarchy is revived for the
occasion.   Louis is seated on his throne, and
remains covered while addressing the assembly in
a short but vague discourse.   In it he seeks to
justify the abandonment to the allies of the ter-
ritorial conquests of the empire.   At the same
time he congratulates the nation on the retention

of those monuments of the valour of the French arms, the grand *chefs d'œuvre* of art, which henceforth, he says, belong to France by rights far more durable and sacred than those of victory. The chancellor, M. d'Ambray, then proceeds, in a long speech, to laud the king and to extol the wisdom of his acts. This is as in the olden time, except that he does not deliver his panegyric humbly kneeling before his sacred majesty; the assembly is not yet sufficiently *pure et simple* in its royalism to tolerate such a revival; therefore the chancellor stands beside the king.

He has now to read this famous Charter, which he announces merely as a decree of legislative reform, in which his majesty condescends to lay down the limits within which he will use the authority he derives from God and his ancestors.

The Charter certainly contained, in form at least, the elements of that liberty which the nation for twenty-five years had been struggling to obtain, and for which it had in 1789 laid the foundation, namely, constitutional monarchy, responsible ministers, immovable judges, equalised taxation assessed by the nation's representatives; individual freedom, every citizen being under the safeguard of the laws; liberty of conscience, and liberty of the press. The last two, the most valued of all, were the first the royalist ministry attempted to modify, or rather nullify, so that they should have no real effect.

The royal Charter, however, guaranteed all these reforms. But saving clauses were adroitly introduced that enabled the monarch to suspend or abolish what he had conceded when it was his *bon plaisir* to do so. Without the promised new constitution the reign of Louis XVIII. would have come to an end almost ere it began. This he well knew, yet could not bring himself — and those about him fostered this feeling — to grant otherwise than as a concession, made of his own free will and royal authority, what the nation claimed as the inalienable rights of citizens.

Had he in good faith acknowledged this claim, the Charter would have been received and appreciated as a real benefit. As it was, it was accepted for what it was worth, which, indeed, was little enough. For, as a French writer (Jouy) remarks, "it cannot be said of Louis XVIII. and his Charter as Montesquieu said of Charlemagne, 'he made excellent laws and regulations, and did even more than that, he compelled them to be observed.'"

But disappointment, from the very outset of the rule of the restored dynasty, was not confined to the political world. Socially, and especially in the life of the court, the ladies, who had looked for a restoration of the elegant dissipation and frivolity of the Marie Antoinette period, also were destined to see their hopes vanish. Ladies of the old nobility who had resided in France during the imperial rule were amazed, and in some few instances slightly shocked and vexed withal, to find how, quite unconsciously, they had fallen into the habits and feelings of those amongst whom they had lived in more or less intimacy during the past ten or twelve years.

This was a grievous thing to confess, even amongst themselves, for it was in some sort like confessing themselves rebel angels fallen from their former high estate. Yet the formal etiquette observed at the Pavillon Marsan, and by the small flock of the faithful who surrounded the Duchesse d'Angoulême, certainly seemed to their perverted minds as wearisome as it was antiquated. The ostentatious piety displayed there was also rather repelling — fasting and prayer, sackcloth and ashes, being the rule, with an anathema for all who cared not to bow to the yoke of the Jesuits.*

The duchess's order prohibiting the wearing of diamonds — afterwards extended to flowers — appeared to be a standing one, so far as it concerned her receptions, which, however, rarely took place, and these were limited to a very small circle. If feathers were worn by herself and permitted to others, it was said to be less from any preference for this head-dress than for the

* Pius VII., by a bull dated August 7, 1814, reëstablished the Company of Jesus, at the pressing entreaties, as he averred, of the bishops, and the unanimous wish of the Catholic world.

purpose of reviving the memory of Marie Antoinette,—of inflicting a penance, as it were, on those
who knew not that unfortunate queen, except as a
chief cause of the miseries of France, but whose
parents may have been guilty of living in 1793.
But feathers in connection with Marie Antoinette
could symbolise nothing but the height of folly in
the extravagant height of her towering head-dresses.

The duchess, however, was supposed not yet
formally to have made her appearance in public,
or to have held a general court reception.   It was
not, in fact, yet fully ascertained who among the
renegades of the old *noblesse* and the converts of
the new were worthy to frequent the sanctimonious court over which she alone was to preside.
She desired to know if the husbands of the ladies
presented to her were of the emigration, and for
how long — was it the emigration of 1789 or
1792? — were they of the army of Condé? etc.   If
resident in France during the "usurpation," had
they held any post in the household of the
"usurper" or his wife? or if converts, had they
at once and unhesitatingly sworn allegiance to
their legitimate sovereign?   These were weighty
questions with the duchess, for, as all black sheep
were to be eliminated from the fold of the Pavillon
Marsan, a sort of *billet de confession* was needed
to obtain the *entrée*.*

* Private letters of 1814 and 1815; also Maréchal Ney's
letters to his wife.

When the wives of any of the marshals, or other suspected persons, made the mistake of paying their respects at the Tuileries, the duchess received them in the most frigid and haughty manner. Her usually severe expression of countenance became severer still, and her harsh voice assumed its harshest tones to dismiss these unwelcome visitors in a manner that plainly forbade further intrusion upon her. Mortified by treatment so humiliating, many ladies left the presence of this narrow-minded, bigoted, revengeful woman, full of indignation and resentment; while others, wounded in feeling and deeply pained by her want of ordinary courtesy towards them, being more emotional, could not restrain their tears. Henceforth, however, both were adversaries, if not bitter enemies, alike of the duchess and her family.

Within the narrow range of the court — if indeed it could be called a court — the influence and authority of the Duchesse d'Angoulême were great and most pernicious. But in the social circles of the capital the influence of woman generally was greater still, and already in certain *salons* the court of the monarchy began to be disparagingly compared with the brilliant one of the empire. Even those ladies of the Faubourg St. Germain who had participated — rather condescendingly, perhaps — in its endless round of festivities, heaved a little sigh of regret when the palmy days of the imperial court, the hunting parties of Fontainebleau, and the gaieties of Compiègne, were mentioned.

Among other intriguing or demonstrative ladies, banished to a distance of thirty or forty leagues from the capital, who hastened to take advantage of Paris being again open to them, was Madame de Staël. The news of Napoleon's defeat and the capitulation of Paris reached her while at a crowded rout in London. She was utterly overcome by emotion, and a succession of paroxysms ensued, first of rapturous delight at the overthrow of her enemy, the man who would not believe in her as an oracle, then of sentimental despondency, lest with the restoration of the monarchy there should be a restoration of old abuses, old prejudices, and the effete forms of the old court etiquette. M. Rocca, her youthful invalid husband, was in dutiful attendance upon her, humble and anxious, and doing his best with *sal volatile, eau de Cologne,* and whispered epithets of endearment to calm the fluttered feelings of his strong-minded wife.

The day after the entry of Louis XVIII. into Paris, Madame de Staël left London. She was desirous of urging her claim on the government of France for two millions of *francs,* deposited by her father in the public treasury, on resigning office, to save the government of Louis XVI. from bankruptcy. Napoleon's millions were fast disappearing ; it was therefore necessary that no time should be lost in making her application ; for to that source alone she looked for payment. Her request for an audience was granted by the king, chiefly, he said, from curiosity. But the duchess was not willing to accede to her wish to pay her court to her. The king, however, decreed that Madame de Staël could not be refused.

He expected, it seems, to find that the twenty-three summers and winters which had passed over Madame de Staël since he last saw her had had the effect of subduing her boisterous energy, her abrupt, almost rude manners, and of improving her personally. Time has indeed an improving effect on some women, and some men too, but within certain limits. Twenty-three years was a long period to go on growing in beauty and refinement. When, therefore, their interview took place, much disappointment was the result. It was not ex-pressed, of course ; the *convenances* did not permit it ; the lady was in the presence of her sovereign, and the sovereign was a man who piqued himself on his extreme politeness and gallantry.

It is the Duc de Doudeauville who relates that Louis was amazed at madame's masculine airs, at the bad taste of her head-dress (the hideous tur-ban she fancied she looked so well in), and at the general eccentricity in her person, her attire, and even her language. The only effect of time on her tongue was increased volubility. It over-

Madame de Stael.
Photo-etching after the painting by Gerard.

powered the king, who preferred to hear himself talk rather than listen to a flow of eloquence in others. Still, she played her part well, managed to bring tears into her bold black eyes, and affected strong emotion. At last she exclaimed, adroitly flattering Louis's pedantry and vanity, "If I only could express myself in Latin, I would recite to the king the Song of Simeon; for, like that holy man, I have now but to die, since I have seen his majesty return to the palace of his ancestors."

"Live, madame; rather live," replied the king, so much delighted that for a moment he seemed disposed to jump up and embrace the lady, unmindful of the dignity which his *rôle* of sovereign by right divine imposed on him. It was probably a sharp twinge of the gout that brought him to his senses, for he contented himself with repeating, "Live, madame, to write of the wonders of this age, and thus ensure them immortality."

"Ah, Sire!" she said, "how different from the Corsican! He would have sent me to my household affairs; but my occupation is the making of books, not shirts. To every one his appointed task. The man's insolence verily killed me with grief."

"That, madame, he could not do," replied the king, "you being immortal."

"Ah, Sire! I recognise in this speech the perfume and flower of French gallantry. The approbation of the king delights me, and emboldens me to say that, if he will sometimes condescend to listen to me, I, who have seen and studied the revolution, can, if the king will allow me, greatly aid him in carrying out his good intentions. Let his majesty consolidate the monarchy. I can give him much useful information, and can recommend men of ability to him — such men as, for instance, M. Constant de Rebecque — for places of trust."

She was about to expatiate on the diplomacy of the period. But she had ventured on dangerous ground ; and Louis, interrupting her in the middle of a fluent tirade, coldly reminded her of the object for which she had asked an audience — the consideration of her claim of two millions on the government. She was annoyed at an interruption which implied the rejection of her services, and assumed a tone which, with the tenor of the letters she subsequently wrote on the subject, was near imperilling the payment of the money.

Benjamin Constant, in one of his letters to Madame Récamier, mentions having prevented Madame de Staël from sending a letter, so arrogant, vehement, and offensive in tone, that it would have certainly produced the rejection of her claim. Eventually, however, she was paid. Napoleon had refused to acknowledge himself responsible for the debt of Louis XVI. ; but the sixty millions he left behind him furnished the

king with the means of payment. "Madame de
Staël," said Louis XVIII. — when referring some
years after to this interview with her — "declared
war against me after 'the hundred days,' because
I did not at her recommendation employ the
Baron Constant de Rebecque, and we were still
in hostility at the time of her death."

Benjamin Constant, as he is more generally
called than Baron Constant de Rebecque, had
been for some years residing in Germany, where
in 1808, when Madame de Staël refused to conse-
crate their *liaison* by becoming his wife, he married Mademoiselle Charlotte von Hardenberg,
daughter of the Prussian Minister, Baron (afterwards Prince) Hardenberg. The lady had pre-
viously been twice married and twice divorced.
Constant himself had undergone that process
once ; but in his second matrimonial venture with
a twice divorced woman he is said to have found a
devoted wife. She, however, did not accompany
him to Paris in 1814. He was to rejoin her in
Brussels, whence they were going to England,
there appearing to be some doubt of Madame
de Constant being well received in the society her
husband frequented in Paris. This seems strange
indeed, as incompatibility of temper is alleged to
have been in both cases the sole cause of the dis-
solution of her marriage ; while the tone of French
society at that period was very far from being
strictly moral.

An instance of this is afforded in that series of passionate love-letters which, at about this time, Constant began to write to Madame Récamier — she a married woman, he a married man. She was accustomed to adoration and homage of that kind, and rather encouraged than repulsed the love-lorn slaves who by the score were sighing out their souls around her. She, too, had just returned to Paris, after three years' absence. Her intimacy with Madame de Staël had displeased Napoleon. It was therefore intimated to her that it would be advisable to reside at some distance from the capital. Without being exactly ordered to do so, she immediately left France, to improve her mind perhaps by foreign travel, as she visited several of the Italian states, finding lovers wherever she went, and passing her time very agreeably.

Though under the ban of Napoleon's displeasure, she was received by Napoleon's sister — Caroline, Queen of Naples — and her husband, Joachim Murat, with the utmost distinction and friendliness. This was at the close of 1813, when, after the battle of Leipzig, Napoleon's downfall seemed imminent. King Joachim, who, as Napoleon said, was a brave soldier but had no moral courage, was then summoned by England and Austria to declare his independence of France and join the coalition, the retention of his kingdom, for which he had stipulated when making advances

to the allies, being on that condition guaranteed
to him by those Powers. His conduct had already
seemed to savour of treachery, yet he hesitated
thus to throw off his allegiance and proclaim himself the ally of the enemies of France and a traitor
to his brother-in-law and benefactor.

During the inward struggle consequent on this
state of mind, he wrote to Napoleon entreating
him to make peace. No reply was vouchsafed.
But Caroline Bonaparte — as fond of power as
Napoleon himself — clung to her royal dignity,
and, supported in her views by Count Metternich,
endeavoured to impress on the vacillating mind of
Joachim that his duty as king superseded all other
considerations. Thus urged, he at last joined the
coalition, and signed the treaty on the 11th of
January, 1814.

No sooner had he done so than it appears he
repented of it; for, when the news was about to
be publicly announced in Naples, he rushed wildly
into his wife's apartment, and finding Madame
Récamier there with the queen, asked her opinion
of the course he ought to take in the dilemma in
which he was placed. She replied (as stated by
herself when relating the circumstance to her
friends), " Sire, you are a Frenchman ; it is to
France you should be faithful." Murat turned
pale, ran to the window, threw it violently open,
and exclaimed, as he pointed to the English fleet
sailing into the bay, " Am I then a traitor ?"

Then, throwing himself on a sofa, he burst into tears.

The queen, though she had far more nerve and strength of mind than her husband, was also greatly agitated. She, however, endeavoured to calm him, and persuaded him to drink a glass of orange-flower water. This seems to have had a soothing effect, as Madame Récamier states that they afterwards drove all over the town, were enthusiastically received, and in the evening appeared at the opera with the Austrian ambassador and the English admiral.

In the autumn of the same year, a few weeks after her return to Paris, — where M. Récamier, having overcome the embarrassments of his former failure, was again a prosperous banker, — Madame Récamier received a letter from the Queen of Naples. Its purport gave her the wished-for opportunity of making some acknowledgment of the friendly attentions and disinterested hospitality she had met with from Murat and his wife. The letter related to Murat's fear of being dispossessed of his kingdom, notwithstanding the guarantee of England and Austria to the contrary. The maintenance of the sovereignties founded by Napoleon was about to be discussed at the Congress, and Murat was desirous of finding some political man of eminence to whom the drawing up of a memorial, setting forth and defending his rights, might be safely confided.

Madame Récamier could think of none so competent as M. Benjamin Constant. She had known him previous to 1807, both in Paris and at Coppet, but as an acquaintance more than a friend. His relations with Madame de Staël, who then dominated him entirely, and the violent scenes that often occurred between them, were unfavourable to the formation of other friendships. But she knew that he had held eminent rank as a brilliant political writer, and that through his intimacy with Madame de Staël he was acquainted with most of the diplomatists of that period, both French and foreign. She wrote to him, therefore, requesting him to call on her, that she might consult him on a matter of some importance.

He came, and Madame Récamier, in the soft accents of that youthful voice she so long retained, explained to him King Joachim's position and wishes. But he, less mindful of the interests of the King of Naples than of the presence of beauty, while he listened with ravished ear to the silvery tones that penetrated to his inmost heart, was scarcely conscious of the import of the words she uttered. His eyes seemed opened for the first time to the fact of her loveliness, and he fell passionately, madly in love with her. He was then forty-seven, she thirty-seven. He undertook the memorial because it was her wish, though, considering his political principles, he could have had little, if any, sympathy with Joachim.

The next day, when sending a draft of it for her perusal, he adds to his note : " Do you know that I have never in the course of my life, already a long one, seen anything in the world equal to you yesterday. I carried your image with me to Beugnot's, to Talleyrand's, to my own home — everywhere in fact. I am dejected because of it. Indeed I do not jest. I am suffering, holding back on the verge of a steep precipice. But it is so indifferent to you to cause suffering of this kind. Ah! angels also have their cruelties. However, for the sake of King Joachim, the memorial must be returned to-day with your own hands. It is a diplomatic duty not to run a risk with it."

This beginning of the strange series of love-letters addressed by him to Madame Récamier is but a very weak specimen compared with the ardour of the later ones. Very rarely did she give any reply to his passionate appeals for a smile, a word of tenderness, of friendship even, such as sometimes she vouchsafed to others whom he termed favoured rivals ; or grant him the ten or five minutes' *tête-à-tête* he so ardently and per-severingly prayed for, telling her she was his god, his heaven, the only being that could influence him for good or evil. Occasionally she wrote him pretty little missives, but did not reject his adora-tion. She rejected none of her train of lovers, though of love she had none to give them, but pitied and smiled and soothed, until, as was said, she had reduced their adoration to friendship, of which she had enough and to spare for all. But Constant complains bitterly of this, as rigour and cruelty; of which it took eighteen months to reduce him to that level. Scarce, however, could he persuade himself to leave her when he could no longer put off rejoining his wife, and on his journey to Brussels he wrote from every place he stopped at.

The memorial with which this love affair originated subsequent events rendered of no avail. But Queen Caroline, on leaving Naples, sent 20,- 000 *francs* and a decoration in diamonds to Benjamin Constant, as a token of her satisfaction with the document and of her gratitude to him. He, however, declined both. The reward he sought was in the smiles of his lady-love, and he certainly risked much to obtain them, putting his liberty and, as most of his friends believed, even his life in jeopardy, though the motive for this extraordinary conduct was then misunderstood; or it was unknown to them.

CHAPTER XI.

THE nation was not long in discovering
that in changing its master it had
made a decided change for the worse.
Its emancipation, as it was termed, from the
despotic sway of the "usurper" had but freed it
from the rule of a man of extraordinary talent,
genius, and activity, to place it under the yoke
of priests and royalist emigrants and a ruler of
mediocre capacity.

It had discovered, too, that the new constitution, so condescendingly bestowed on it, was, in
fact, but a mere delusion and a snare. Like the
utterances of the famous oracles of old, its articles
were susceptible of a double interpretation, and,
thus ingeniously constructed and administered
according to the ideas of the partisans of the

right divine, served, as a weapon of offence and
defence, for carrying out the purposes of the king
and his ministry. Discontent was therefore general
and anxiety daily increasing. Longing eyes began
to be turned towards Elba — and not only by old
soldiers of the imperial army, now incorporated
with the new levies, and compelled, sorely against
the grain, regularly to confess, and to attend mass
far more frequently than parade. They, at times,
would soothe their ruffled feelings by many a
muttered "*Morbleu!*" or risk being put under
arrest by raising the cry, irresistibly as it seemed,
of "*Vive l'empereur!*"

The Duc de Berry, who so far resembled his
men that he swore like a trooper and went to
mass and confession only when he could not avoid
it, was one day reviewing the grenadier guards,
when, instead of "*Vive le roi!*" an outburst of
"*Vive l'empereur*" was raised by some of the
old guards scattered amongst the new regiment.

"What the devil does this mean?" cried the
duke in a rage, and adding to his invocation to the
devil a formidable oath. "What is it that attaches
you," he continued to rave on, "to this confounded
Corsican fellow? He dragged you all over Europe,
and never even gave you your pay."

"Didn't he," answered one of the men, in a
tone that seemed to say, "Indeed he did."
"But," he went on, "if we chose to give him
credit, *sacré!* what is that to you?"

The duke is said to have laughed outright, and to have received a *viva* for it, which may possibly have toned down the wrath of this arrogant and fiery little duke, and saved the men from the punishment due to a breach of discipline.

But discontent was not confined to the army. Even among the partisans of the monarchy there were complaints of the incompetency and imbecility of the government. Much disgust was also inspired by Louis's constant harping on the "right divine and the 19th year of his reign." * A coronation and its accompanying festivities, by amusing the public mind, might perhaps for a time have veiled from it the political inaptitude of the king and his newly formed ministry. But Pius VII., who crowned Napoleon, absolutely refused to recognise the pretension of Louis XVIII. to date his reign from the death, in 1795, of the young dauphin called Louis XVII.

His holiness was reminded that in crowning Napoleon he had acted under compulsion. He, however, utterly rejected such a suggestion. No constraint, he said, had been put on him. It was of his own free will he came to Paris to crown the man whom the nation had chosen; and he declared that Napoleon was duly consecrated, anointed with the holy oil, recognised by the sovereigns of Europe as of the brotherhood of kings, and was as legitimately a sovereign prince

* M. de Jaucourt in " *Talleyrand Correspondance.*"

as the rest. This was an unexpected and morti-
fying rebuff to the "right divine," and in vain
Louis talked of reuniting the separated links of
the chain of time, of blotting from his memory,
as he would wish to blot from the page of history,
what had occurred in his kingdom during his
absence — especially the reign of Napoleon, of
course. But for the blotting out of that, the fiat
of the Pope could have availed him nothing.

In default, then, of the coronation, which was
to have been a grand and imposing spectacle, a
splendid revival of the ancient ceremonial of the
cortège of the Corpus Christi, or *Fête Dieu*, was
announced. This ecclesiastical pageant had not
been seen in France since 1788, and for several
previous years had been shorn of much of its
former pomp. Already an army of foreign priests
had arrived. They seemed to have awaited only
the evacuation of the capital by the allies to enter
and take possession. Masses, prayers, processions, and sermons were now the order of the
day ; and everywhere Monsieur and his elder son
and the duchess were attended by a retinue of
bishops, *curés*, and *abbés* — part of the numerous
staff of their ecclesiastical households.

The Palace of St. Cloud, inhabited lately by
Prince Schwarzenberg and suite, was now given
in part by the king to his brother, who established a colony of priests therein, and made it the
headquarters of these new invaders. The princes,

often expected, but rarely ever seen, at the theatres, with the exception of the Duc de Berry, might almost daily be found prostrate in prayer before the image of some saint in one or other of the churches, or on their knees communicating in public. The people regarded these mummeries, some with mocking eye, others with indignation. The king himself, in his younger days a professed *esprit fort*, and still affecting to pique himself on fidelity to the principles of the philosophy of the eighteenth century, smiled derisively on the practices of the Pavillon Marsan and its open parade of the forms of piety. But he was far from desiring to oppose what was, in fact, "part of a system of restoration then being applied to all Catholic states, where religion then became an efficacious means of moral government."

The king's infirmities, naturally, did not allow him, had he even been inclined, to take any part in the procession of the *Fête Dieu*. The glory of accompanying it, bareheaded and on foot, through the principal streets of Paris, was therefore reserved for Monsieur and his two sons. The burly Angoulême, with downcast eyes and solemn air, was on his right; the sprightly pygmy De Berry, scarcely restraining his extreme vexation, yet making excellent use of his *beaux yeux*, as he tramped along, was on the left. But the ladies who filled the balconies on the line of march awarded the palm to the Comte d'Artois, despite his age, for grace and personal elegance. The duchess, with two of her ladies of honour, followed in a carriage, and was saluted with cries of *"A bas les prêtres! à bas les Jésuites!"* The people detested her, believing her to be the chief cause, as to a great extent she was, of this gradual resurrection of the old priest-ridden times. The street processions of the Church alarmed the children of the revolution, and they murmured loudly; for the *Fête Dieu* was not the first, and others were to follow, particularly that of the Vow of Louis XIII., in honour of the Holy Virgin, under whose protection he placed his kingdom.

The king had formed his household, domestic and military, precisely on the same plan as that to which Louis XVI. succeeded but which he afterwards greatly modified. Again the "Maison rouge" included the *chevaux légers*, the *gardes du corps*, and black and gray *mousquetaires*. The Swiss regiments were to be reorganised and added to the military *cortège* which composed the king's escort, and served rather for show and parade than use. The army itself was neglected, for the Bourbons thought that by placing the Throne, as they said, on the sure foundation of the Altar, there would be no further need for unsheathing the sword of France—at all events while Louis, and after him Charles, perchance, should sit on it.

Their flatterers told them they were the masters of the future no less than of the present;

and M. de Châteaubriand, considered the oracle of royalty, declared in the Senate that "the king was now so strong, so firmly seated, that no human power could shake his throne." The younger military men perceived regretfully that their career was ended, that the army no longer offered prizes to stimulate valour, that even the cross of the Legion of Honour, which it was once their ambition to win, was now systematically degraded — flung, as it were, contemptuously to any who chose to pick it up and wear it. True, the Bonapartists looked on it with some disdain as a mere counterfeit, since its eagle had given place to the *fleur-de-lys*, and the bust of the emperor to that of Henri IV. The slight put on the " Corsican's Order" was, however, one of the minor causes of irritation among the imperialist opponents of the Bourbon dynasty.

The proposal of the obsequious royalist Senate and Chamber of Deputies that his majesty should be " humbly supplicated" to name the amount of the debts he had contracted during *his absence* from his kingdom, raised an outcry from the constitutionalists, in which the republican and revolutionary parties loudly joined ; for thirty-three millions of *francs* had just been voted for his civil list ; he had had in ready cash Napoleon's sixty millions, all the royal palaces newly and sumptuously furnished, the capital improved and embellished, useful public works completed, many additions to the crown jewels, and "during his absence" he had been pensioned by Russia and England at the rate of 24,000*l.* a year. The king, however, was graciously pleased to name thirty millions as the amount of his debts, and that sum was immediately voted for their payment. But it appears that they really amounted to a much larger sum, which was chiefly paid in places and pensions. As for those creditors to whom payment in that way was impracticable, they were treated after the manner of the old *régime* — left unpaid. But, with persistent impertinence, they were often knocking at the door of the Tuileries — unavailingly of course. In the good old times the claims of these clamorous people would have been settled at once by a *lettre de cachet* and a lodging in the Bastille. Now, alas! this convenient way of getting rid of troublesome customers (more correctly creditors in the instance in question) was not available; yet means were found during the reign of these Bourbons as quietly and effectually to dispose of people who for reasons great or small, well or ill founded, made themselves obnoxious to the king or the government.

On the 17th of October the deputy Dumolard remarked, with reference to the projects of the priestly party headed by the Comte d'Artois and the Duc and Duchesse d'Angoulême, that "to pretend to restore the past and destroy the pres-

ent was to attempt the impossible, and could lead
only to further confusion and fresh political con-
vulsions." A law was under discussion for re-
storing to the emigrants the yet unsold estates
confiscated as national property. There were a
few dissentient voices, but the law was passed.
It was, however, but a preliminary measure, it
being the king's declared intention, as the minister, Comte Ferrand, a fanatical royalist, informed
the Chamber, that restitution should be made to
the clergy and nobility of the lands of which they
had been despoiled.

Declared national property in 1790, they had
passed since then by purchase into various hands.
A large portion was owned by small agricultural
proprietors, amongst whom Comte Ferrand's announcement created much agitation, and increased
the extreme antipathy with which in their hearts
they already regarded the Bourbons. Regret for
the emperor became general among them, and in
some vague sort of way they placed their hopes in
him and looked for his return. Thus, after six
months of the Bourbon rule, the imperialist reaction set in, and the souvenirs of the empire and
the tri-coloured banner, needing no emissaries to
revive them, rose up in protest against all that
had been done in France since the restoration of
the monarchy in April.

The peasantry had often cursed the long wars
of the empire, and perhaps the emperor himself,

yet had never refused him his impost of blood. Being menaced in the possession of their property, they now cursed Louis XVIII., his emigrant court, his priests, and his devotees, and with a far bitterer curse. They would have given their last *sou* and last *franc* to the " Petit Caporal," who gained such splendid victories, who distributed crosses of honour on the battle-field, and had made marshals of France of the sons of men who had followed the plough. But they were firmly resolved to yield not an acre of land, or an iota of their rights of proprietorship, to that *"gros goutteux"* (as Louis was generally called by the people) who had been brought back to France by the Cossacks.* Prints and small images of Napoleon and his eagle, sold by the pedlars at fairs and markets, again adorned the cottage and farmhouse shelves and walls, and were conspicuously placed in the workshops.

But opposition towards the restored dynasty was most strongly displayed in determined resistance to the tyrannical pretensions of the priesthood. Secret associations existed in the army, a sort of freemasonry whose rallying word was the name of Napoleon ; while in social circles the violet was adopted as an emblem of imperialism, and the device, " It will reappear in the spring," told of the hopes of its partisans.

That singular personage, Madame de Krüdener,

* P. Lacroix.

who was then striving to imbue Parisian society
with her mystical doctrines, and who afterwards
so greatly influenced the mind of the Emperor
Alexander, added to the hopes and fears of those
who had faith in her the weight of a, so called,
prophecy.   There certainly was nothing remarkable in predicting the event of which most people
had a presentiment; especially as she was no
stranger to the fact that intriguers of the imperialist party were diligently exerting themselves to
bring about that event, and that the acts of the
Bourbons were well calculated to hasten its
realisation.

But the prophetess laid claim to divine inspiration, the purposes of the Almighty, as she averred,
being spiritually communicated to her.   She had
greatly desired to throw her spell over her imperial countryman, "God having revealed to her
that a splendid mission was in store for him."
But opportunity seems to have been wanting for
carrying out her designs on the czar during the
agitated period of the first invasion.   The many
conflicting interests, political and otherwise, of the
various sections of Parisian society, absorbed public attention far more than Madame de Krüdener's
mission to preach repentance to a sinful generation and to inculcate the doctrine of pure love.
She had adopted the views of Madame Guyon, and
believed herself "selected by the Eternal" to carry
on the work of that visionary ; its completion being

destined for another female apostle whom Heaven, she said, would raise up in the early years of the next century.

Madame de Krüdener's teachings were but coldly received by the ladies of the Parisian *beau monde*. "She is a good woman," said the Duchesse de Saint-Leu, "but I comprehend nothing of her doctrines." Madame Récamier, *si impressionnable*, as she describes herself, listened unmoved to her mystical rhapsodies, though declaimed with some eloquence. Had she been drawn within the mystic circle, her *cortège* of lovers would doubtless have been drawn too, and Madame de Krüdener's disciples increased by a host of political celebrities, men of literary eminence, the most distinguished of the military heroes then in Paris, Wellington himself included. But Madame de Récamier, herself a sort of rival priestess, inspiring love but not preaching it, and accepting only the homage of friendship, was by no means willing that those slaves who came under the sway of her own sceptre should be transferred to that of Madame de Krüdener.

It was during the Congress of Vienna that, following up her designs on Alexander, Madame de Krüdener wrote to Mdlle. Stourdza, an enthusiast of similar views, and after strongly condemning the festivities in which the assembly of emperors, kings, princes, and ambassadors passed their time, proceeded mysteriously to announce the return of

Napoleon, for the chastisement of the allies and the punishment of guilty France, as decreed by the Eternal. " Those lilies," she wrote, "those pure and fragile emblems which God preserved and willed that they should break an iron sceptre — those lilies that should have called France to repentance, to purity, to love of God — have appeared only again to disappear. The lesson is given, and men, more hardened than before, dream only of tumult. The storm is advancing, and we should tremble at the approach of this dreaded time, of which all have the presentiment, though not the certainty."

Mdlle. Stourdza thought this " prophecy " sufficiently wonderful and alarming to be communicated to the Emperor Alexander, whom Madame de Krüdener, as she knew, was very desirous of seeing, expecting to find in him, in some sort, a kindred spirit. She afterwards added to her prophecy: " A great epoch is approaching. All is about to be overthrown — schools, human science, states, thrones! The children of God are about to be assembled. The end of the world is at hand!" This she proclaimed in Paris at one of her mystical séances.

But neither the king, his family, nor his ministry were roused to any sense of approaching danger by the menacing attitude of a dissatisfied people and an army scarce restrained from open revolt ; much less, then, could the preachings of

Madame de Krüdener trouble the repose of royalty, even if they reached its august ears. Louis XVIII. was then arranging his monthly receptions of ladies of the court. They were to begin with the new year. His chief advisers in this important matter were his old favourite and friend in exile, M. Blacas-d'Aulps, now minister of his household, and the fascinating Comtesse du Cayla. But little assistance did he receive from the Duchesse d'Angoulême. She however frowned her disapproval of the king's levity when he remarked, on the list of ladies eligible for the honour in preparation for them being handed to him, " I object to none who are pretty, amiable, lively, and witty ;" an expressive glance telling the fair countess that those pleasing qualities were united in her.

The Comtesse Zoé du Cayla had already had several mysterious *tête-à-tête* interviews with the king, and orders were given to admit her whenever she presented herself. So great a favour caused much uneasiness to M. Blacas, who at that time was especially careful to allow no one to approach the king whose influence seemed likely to diminish his own. But the king had conceived so strong a friendship for this lady that his old favourite was obliged to yield, and once or twice in the week respectfully to withdraw from the royal presence when a small concealed door in the king's apartment was opened, and his confidential *valet de chambre* introduced the countess. Gout interfered greatly with Louis's disposition to display his gallantry towards the fair sex. It tied him to his armchair. But although he could not rise to receive the lady he honoured with his preference, he was profuse of compliments, his sudden animation testifying to the reality of the pleasure her visit afforded him, as a break in the dreary monotony of his life.

She was the daughter of M. Talon, one of the king's advocates of the Châtelet, to whom a principal part was assigned in the instructions respecting the affair of the unfortunate Comte de Favras, whom Louis XVIII., then Comte de Provence — to save himself from public reproach — so basely abandoned. Papers very compromising to the Comte de Provence came into the hands of Madame du Cayla on the death of her father. When Louis became king he entreated her to burn them, and in his presence. She consented, and for this act was munificently rewarded. At the breaking out of the revolution her father emigrated, but returned to France during the Consulate. He had the rare good fortune to find his property unsold, and to receive it back intact. He then placed his daughter at Madame Campan's establishment, where she formed a friendship with Hortense de Beauharnais, whose lady-in-waiting she afterwards became when Queen of Holland. Under the empire suspicion fell on M. Talon as an agent of the Bourbons, and he was imprisoned;

but, aided by her friend and schoolfellow, his daughter succeeded in obtaining his release. This persecution, as it was called, together with Mdlle. Talon's marriage with the Comte du Cayla, a royalist (from whom, however, she soon separated), and her services as secret agent of the intriguers of the Faubourg St. Germain and the exile of Hartwell, ensured her a favourable reception at the court of the Restoration. Her journeys to England in 1813 and 1814 were made *viâ* Holland, under the pretence of seeking change of air for her health. The Duc de Rovigo (Général Savary), then Minister of Police, furnished her with a passport, being a man of much gallantry when not called on in the exercise of the duties of his office to employ severity, and he seems to have been persuaded that no occasion existed for it in this case. She frequented both imperialist and royalist *salons*, and still kept up her intimacy with the ex-queen. But towards the end of 1814 Madame du Cayla informed the king that men inimical to his government might be constantly met with at the *réunions* of the Duchesse de Saint-Leu.

Louis affected to treat this information with indifference. He pressed the soft white hand and kissed the fingers of the fair informant, quoted a Latin phrase or two, and bade her eschew politics. But he was extremely vexed, notwithstanding ; for had he not made a real duchess of this sham

ex-queen? This by all laws human and divine
should have bound her, in gratitude, to him forever. The Comte Blacas-d'Aulps, who made a
point of never telling his sacred majesty anything
that could ruffle his temper, was much annoyed at
the *maladresse* of the king's new favourite. But
he took the precaution of authorising Général
Clarke, in default of vigilance on the part of the
Prefect of Police, to keep a watchful eye on the
proceedings of the Duchesse de Saint-Leu and her
clique.

The general probably did not care to accept
the post of spy, or at least to be very vigilant in
performing its duties, for when the anxious M.
Blacas asked for the result of his espionage, he
informed him that the Duchesse de Saint-Leu's
soirées were simply musical *réunions*.

"But the secret conferences, General?"

"Merely rehearsals, M. le Comte, rehearsals of
acted charades in preparation for the evening's
amusement."

M. Blacas was satisfied, and when next Madame
du Cayla visited the king, before she was ushered
into the royal presence, he took her aside and
begged her not to agitate his majesty by reports
which really had no foundation. What she had
suspected to be secret conferences, were but private rehearsals of charades, or some pastimes of
that kind. In that true light she would in future,
he trusted, regard them.

Yet these acted charades are said to have been closely connected with events that eventually brought about that of "the hundred days;" for Hortense had great influence, and used it actively on Napoleon's behalf.

CHAPTER XII.

HE order that no diamonds, no flowers,
nor ornaments of any kind, except
feathers, be worn at the court of the
Tuileries was rescinded with the arrival of the
new year, 1815. The Duchesse d'Angoulême
then made her first announced public appearance,
and in a very resplendent *toilette* of rich pearl-
tinted velvet, elaborately trimmed with antique
point-lace. The stomacher of her dress was entirely covered with diamonds, the sleeves were
profusely ornamented with them, and a *rivière* of
the same brilliant gems sparkled in her hair.

Her earrings were those worn by the Empress
Joséphine at her coronation. They were formed
of two magnificent pear-shaped brilliants within a
circle of fine yellow diamonds. Formerly they
had belonged to Marie Antoinette, but during the
revolution were bought by one of the court jewellers, of whom, by order of Napoleon, they were
purchased for the empress for 250,000 *francs*
(10,000*l.*). It was in this way, probably, that
they again became part of the crown jewels;
otherwise Joséphine, who had a weakness for such
ornaments, would surely have added them to the
endless treasures she already possessed of that
kind.

The occasion honoured with so dazzling a display was one scarcely worthy of it — the revival
of the old custom of royalty dining in public.
With it was also reintroduced the "right of the
tabouret." This was plainly marking the distinction between the empire and the monarchy,
these customs having formed no part of the court
etiquette of the former. The spectacle of a
Bourbon indulging his enormous appetite could,
however, under any circumstances, hardly be
considered a pleasing one, even when, as on the
occasion in question, it was at a *banquet aux
grands couverts* served in the superbly restored
Hall of Diana. "The table groaned," as the
phrase is, under the weight of the magnificently
wrought imperial gold plate, to which, among

many other of the Corsican's treasures, the lucky
Bourbons succeeded.

Notwithstanding that dining in public was in
some sort a custom of the old *régime*, yet several
of the descendants of the sainted Louis IX. had
seen fit to honour it more in the breach than the
observance, and even entirely to abolish it during
their rule. Saint Louis himself dined frequently
in public with his chiefs and retainers around him,
the pious mendicant monks this monarch encouraged carrying away the ample remnants of the
feast, and the dogs of the company eating up the
crumbs that fell under the rustic board beneath
the famous shady oak of Vincennes; where,
besides his dining-table, the saintly king established also his Court of Justice.

During the four centuries intervening between
the reigns of Louis the Saint and Louis the *Grand
Monarque* the custom was suppressed or revived
according to the mood of the reigning monarch.
The magnificent Louis XIV. never ate in the
presence of an admiring public. He required for
his sustenance as much food as five strong men
of hearty appetite could consume, and alone and
in solemn state he devoured it — very wisely, too,
for the godlike attributes ascribed to him by
himself and his courtiers forbade that ordinary
mortals, or even his mistresses — except when
he trifled with his favourite strawberries and
sweet apple-puffs between his regular meals —

should gaze on his godship feeding, not, as might be imagined, on ambrosia, but on the savoury contents of a goodly array of well-filled dishes.

Louis XV., who was a clever cook, generally preferred to dine *tête-à-tête* with his *maîtresse-en-titre*, or, when in more hilarious mood, with a chosen few of his courtiers, a *vol-au-vent* of his own making forming part of the repast. Yet the "Well-beloved" was not averse to his faithful lieges looking on while at his morning meal he expertly, and at one fell stroke, cut off the top of one 'or more eggs and sent them flying to the end of the table; afterwards, with much apparent enjoyment, eating the yolks with a plateful of nicely cut sippets of toasted bread.

Louis XVI. thought to gratify the people by the frequent sight of their monarch and his family dining or supping. All unconscious on those occasions of the many eyes — often mocking and contemptuous ones — that were fixed upon him, he was intent only on devouring the large portions of food that were set before him. But Marie Antoinette, more quick to perceive the mocking glance and the generally unfavourable impression created by the repulsive habits of her royal spouse on the spectators of this scene, was so much disgusted with her liege lord, and impatient of the restraint imposed on her by the wearisome length of the ceremony, that she was rarely present at these public banquets. The "right of the tabouret" she may be said to have virtually abolished when she bade all the ladies of the court standing around her sit down in her presence, irrespective of rank — the unprivileged baronesses and countesses together with the privileged and indignant duchesses.

Louis XVIII. was probably more repulsive to look upon when dining in public than his unfortunate brother. The latter, notwithstanding his great corpulency for so young a man, could at all events walk to his well-spread board and take his seat without aid. But Louis XVIII., together with the chronic gout that afflicted him, had acquired, as years rolled on, an unwieldy bulk that was positively startling. Many country people, who came to Paris expressly to see their new king, gazed on him with the utmost awe. This, in his amazing vanity, he mistook for personal admiration, for he imagined himself a model of manly beauty. There were ladies who, to gain his favour — and of course some substantial proof of it for themselves or their friends — did not scruple, in pretty perfumed *billets doux*, to tell him so.

"They compliment him" (says a letter from Paris) "on his lovely complexion, which pleases him almost as much as Madame du Cayla's flattering amazement at the depth of his learning and the pungency of his Attic wit. Certainly his face is florid enough, if that be beauty, large and round too, and, with his peculiar manner of wearing his hair, very like the pictures on signboards of the rising sun. But this florid appearance is due to the surgical skill and anxious watchfulness of the Père Élisée, who endeavours to ward off apoplexy, and to subdue the natural effects of the insatiable gluttony of his royal patient, without subduing the gout — the penalty of his want of moderation. *That* Élisée dare not deliver him from if he could." * But his majesty's dinner is waiting.

Usually the king was wheeled into the banqueting-room. On his first appearance he decides to walk. Supported by his Hartwell cane (a cherished souvenir of his exile), and leaning heavily on the arm of the first gentleman of the chamber, he contrives to reach the centre of the large horseshoe table, and is then placed comfortably in his armchair. On his right sits the stern, unsympathetic Duchesse d'Angoulême; on his left Monsieur le Comte d'Artois, with his "august son" Angoulême beside him; and on the right of the "illustrious duchess" sits Monseigneur the Duc de Berry.

On each side of the table, at a distance of two or three feet from the scene of action, is ranged a row of folding seats without backs, *les tabourets*. On them are seated the duchesses of ancient stock, together with the scarcely tolerated *parvenues*, all in full court costume. The royal

* Private letters of 1814 and 1815.

party being small, these ladies have the advantage of uninterrupted contemplation of his "sacred majesty's" and his august family's unequalled prowess in the demolition of all that comes before them.

The king's favourite dish of fifteen mutton cutlets — all of which, *sautées au jus*, he daily despatches at breakfast, and again at dinner, varied by a *sauce à la champagne* — appears as usual, and as usual soon disappears.

A light railing, breast high, extends along the gallery at the foot of the table at which royalty is regaling itself, the repast lasting long enough for ten thousand people to pass before this barrier and to get a glimpse of their new masters.   Much curiosity is said to have been displayed, but no indication was perceived of affectionate interest. Expressions of disappointment there were at the absence of the Duc d'Orléans, whom many expected to see there.   Nor was it quite comprehended that his title not being *royal* but merely *serene* was a valid reason for his exclusion.

The duke himself was annoyed, and commented on the barrier raised between royalty and the *people*, it suiting him thus to proclaim himself one of them.   But Louis XVIII., who in his youth had designs on his brother's throne, seemed thoroughly to understand the *rusé* character of the serene cousin who was lying in wait for his. It was with a sort of malicious pleasure, too, that he constantly refused him the much-coveted title of Royal Highness.

The attempted revival of obsolete forms and customs, of old-world etiquette, and, in a certain sense, the deification of royalty by again surrounding it with the trappings of the effete old *régime*, met with sympathy only from extreme royalists, emigrants, and turncoats. They hoped to profit by this retrograde movement, which gradually was to carry them back to the good old times when both Church and state ruled with absolute sway.

The reign of Louis XVIII. has been called "a despotism tempered by songs and epigrams." In France, indeed, the *chanson*, the epigram, and vaudeville have at all periods of its history been employed to express public opinion and to avenge an abuse of power, as well as to satirise the fashions, follies, and vices of society, and to proclaim the joy of the people. "Never, probably," says De Jouy, "since the foundation of the French monarchy, could a law, an edict, an ordinance, be named, which was not forthwith put into couplets and sung." Thus the levity and lightheartedness of the people would seem to be never wholly repressible, even under political oppression, national troubles, and the deprivation of national liberty.

The restoration of the monarchy afforded a fertile field and ample scope for the exercise of the *chansonnier's* powers. It was then that Désaugiers and Béranger (the *chansonnier par excellence*) produced several of their most famous ditties. "Béranger, in some of his compositions, has risen to the height of lyric poetry. He was more varied, fertile, and correct than his rival Désaugiers, or any of his predecessors in the same style; and possessed in a greater degree the talent of mocking gracefully, bantering wittily, and of rendering folly and vanity supremely ridiculous. Throughout his most frolicsome songs, his love of country is perceptible, and, as it were, a melancholy smile which adds a charm to the gaiety itself." *

Béranger's "*Marquis de Carabas*" diverted the public greatly, while it gave much annoyance to the royalist emigrants. Their claims and pretensions, on returning to France with the Bourbons, are keenly ridiculed in the person of the famous Marquis of Perrault's tale of Puss-in-Boots. His clever cat — his sole possession — had obtained for him numerous wide domains, of which the marquis, on returning from emigration, demands restitution, together with all the privileges of the *noblesse* of the old *régime*. This political satire was aimed at the law of restitution.

Béranger was considered unapproachable in the political *chanson*. In jovial ditties, Désaugiers sometimes equalled, if he did not quite surpass him, though he was rarely so happy in the choice of his subject. But Béranger could always reach

* M. de Jouy.

the hearts of the people, and in *" Le Vieux Soldat"*
he revived enthusiasm for Napoleon when the sentiment in many minds was beginning to wane.

The theatres also played their part in keeping
green the memory of the exiled hero.   Though
many of the actors and actresses had become zealous Bourbonites, several yet remained stanch im·
perialists ; and any sentence, in the play they were
performing, that seemed to convey an allusion to
the absent chief, did not lose its full effect for
want of due emphasis.   Hisses or applause followed, according to the predominating sentiment
of the audience.

Amongst theatrical celebrities of that day none
was more distinguished, both for talent and beauty,
than Mdlle. Mars.   She was an enthusiastic ad-
mirer of Napoleon, and did not scruple openly to
avow it.   By way of expressing this feeling, as
well as her antipathy to the Bourbons who had
supplanted her hero, she one day, when informed
that the king had reëstablished the long disbanded
ornamental regiments of household troops, replied
by the witty *calembour*, " Mars and the *gardes du
corps* have nothing in common."   This, being
whispered about, reached the ears of some of
those valiant carpet-knights, who are said to have
winced terribly under the disdainful sentence
passed on them by the beautiful and *spirituelle*
actress.   But when Madame du Cayla repeated it
to the king, he was much amused ; and gallantry,

of course, forbade him to allow that a lady, young, lovely, and witty, should be reproved — as was expected — for what was termed her indiscretion.

The violets were then beginning to appear, and Mdlle. Mars, like many of Napoleon's partisans, wore in her dress the modest symbolic flower that had become the adversary of the stately lily, and, with the *tricolor*, was under the ban of proscription. " The French Thalia " was immensely popular, and deservedly so; but when she appeared at the Théâtre Français as Célimène, in " *Tartuffe*," with a bouquet of violets in her dress, it was thought even by some of her admirers that she presumed too much on her favour with the public. Opponents of the government, however, vehemently applauded what they regarded as her courage ; whilst the royalists who were present — and among them, it appears, were some of the *gardes du corps* — determined that she should expiate her former offence and present audacity by sacrificing her violets to the cry of " *Vive le roi !* "

But Célimène turned a deaf ear to this demand. A great commotion ensued, and the performance was interrupted. At last turning to the audience, she said, " I have spoken the words." " No one has heard them," was the reply ; " speak them again, and louder." But this she would not do. " Go on with the play," she said, addressing the actors then on the stage. And, strangely enough, the disturbance, which but a few minutes before seemed likely to become a serious one, by some mysterious influence was suddenly quelled. The performance was continued without further interruption; the fair Célimène triumphantly wearing her violets to the end, and receiving enthusiastic applause. This peaceful termination of a threatened riot was believed to be due to a private and authoritative order to the *gardes du corps* to tone down the vehemence of their wounded feelings— an *émeute* on such grounds being by no means desirable.

However, a ceremony was then in preparation which by its great solemnity was intended to overawe the public mind and bring a repentant nation to its knees. As it was to take place chiefly in Paris, it was thought well to avoid embittering the feelings of the Parisian people by squabbles which, insignificant in their origin, might, as was so often the case, develop into factious demonstrations very difficult to put down. The ceremony referred to was the public royal funeral announced to take place on the 21st of January. The few fragments of human bones — supposed to be those of Louis XVI. and Marie Antoinette — found in a corner of the old cemetery of the Madeleine, were then to be conveyed in solemn state to St. Denis, and deposited in one of the now vacant niches of the royal vault.

It was stipulated by one of the secret clauses of the Treaty of Paris that royalty having lost much

of its prestige in France by the execution of the
king, some striking reparation should be made
to it.   To accord the honours of a royal funeral to
the ashes of Louis XVI. would cast a stigma, it
was thought, on the vote which condemned him to
death ; and being conceded in this way, and on
the anniversary of his execution, would be, in fact,
an open recantation of it — a sort of *amende ho-
norable* to the monarch, and at the same time the
reinstating of his memory.   The public, however,
did not regard it in this light.

Already, on the 10th of April, 1814, a very
grand ceremony, military and religious, had taken
place on the Place Louis Quinze, as an atonement,
and a purification of the spot where the king and
queen died on the scaffold.   All the grandees then
in Paris, Protestant and Catholic, attended.   Chief
among them were the Emperor Alexander, his
brother, and principal officers.   The officiating
priest was of the Greek Church.   The service
concluded with a benediction and the presentation
of the cross to the emperor, who having kissed it,
the priest handed it around to the rest.   The
Grand Duke Constantine then raised his hat
as a signal, and Paris resounded with salvos of
artillery.

This tribute to the memory of the unfortunate
pair who brought so much misery on others who
perished on that blood-stained spot, as well as on
themselves, might have been thought sufficient by

those who came proclaiming forgetfulness of the
past. But in reality they had nothing but the
past in their minds. Louis XVIII., uninfluenced
by his pious brother and devout, revengeful niece,
doubtless would have desired no further ceremony.
None gave him credit for any deep feeling in the
matter ; indeed, it was well known that he had
none. He had done his best to add to the
troubles of poor, weak Louis XVI., and to asperse
the character of his wife, and amongst his partisans none had sought to justify him.

Yet, with a view of imparting some sort of
reality to this mock royal funeral, the king sent
for the executioner Sanson, who was conducted
into the sovereign's presence with every appearance of mystery, though care was taken that all in
the palace should know who was his visitor. Sanson was closely questioned respecting the spot
where the head and body of the king were thrown.
It was a wide, deep trench in the old churchyard,
and not dug for him alone. Other victims of
those terrible times — men and women, their
heads and headless bodies *pêle-mêle* — were tossed
there together, and covered over with quicklime.

Nine months elapsed between the execution of
the king and that of the queen, and during that
time hundreds, or rather thousands, of victims
perished. It was not likely, therefore, that their
bodies lay in the same pit. Many trenches had
been dug and filled, many cartloads of lime been

needed — if but to prevent a pestilence in that city of blood and crime. Seven *francs* were paid, too, as the public accounts attested, for a deal coffin and a cushion of lime for "the widow Capet." Twenty-three years after, Sanson was summoned to point out the spot which, to the best of his recollection, was the grave of that most unfortunate yet most blameworthy royal pair.

The search was ordered, and the two persons who then owned the land, together with eight gentlemen of the court, were appointed to witness the proceeding and to identify the remains. All that was discovered, after the most diligent turning over of the soil, consisted of a few yet unconsumed fragments of human bones, and some scraps of woollen stuff and other material mixed up with the dust and ashes of the bodies, a part of whose clothing they once had been. Further to testify that these *triste* remains were really those of human beings, yet a portion of a skull was found, which M. de Châteaubriand — one of the royalist witnesses — declared to be that of Marie Antoinette!

"I recognise it," he said, "by the remembrance I retain of the sweet and gracious smile I received from that head when presented at the court of Versailles!"

Ah! what grim folly! It makes one shudder!

None, however, gave credence to M. de Châteaubriand's assertion. It was ascribed to the vanity and affectation so characteristic of him. But it satisfied M. Blacas, who reported the discovery to the king. He was as unbelieving as others ; but his family and their priestly coterie at least affected to believe, and "the remains" were collected and placed in a splendid coffin. The people of Paris were greatly incensed. The most moderate declared that absence from the ceremony should form their public protest against it. Others were exasperated and indignant beyond measure, and it was fortunate, perhaps, that an opportunity occurred of openly showing their displeasure, and in a manner that seemed in some sort appropriate.

The celebrated tragic actress Mdlle. Raucourt died at that time. She had retired from the stage for many years, and employed her large fortune in acts of benevolence. Also she left in her will a legacy of considerable amount to the Church, which was accepted, for distribution to the poor of her parish. She was generally much respected, and when her funeral took place a very numerous *cortège* assembled to accompany it to St. Roch. On arriving at the church the doors were found closed, the *curé* refusing to allow the body to be brought into the sacred edifice, actors and actresses under the old *régime* being denied the rites of the Church.

Under the empire this was not the case. But of course it was supposed that the Charter, with its guarantee of freedom of worship and equal rights, included the right of Christian burial to all; just as it was supposed to have thrown a veil over those painful memories which, by the funeral, the fasting, and prayers announced for the 21st, it now was sought to revive, in order to further the designs of despotism and priestcraft. Submit to this tyranny the people vehemently declared they would not. The corpse of the actress was more worthy of religious rites than the refuse of the old churchyard collected in the royal coffin, and Christian burial it should have.

No attention, however, being given to the demand that the doors of St. Roch be opened to admit the funeral *cortège* of Mdlle. Raucourt, a great commotion ensued. Several hundred persons had joined the already numerous assemblage, and, amid cries of indignation, an attack on the massive church doors began. At length they yielded; and, just as the newly formed Swiss regiment appeared on the scene to disperse the assailants, the coffin was borne triumphantly into the church. Very fortunately also — or a disgraceful riot might have ensued — two priests were there, and appeared to be waiting the approach of the coffin. Unhesitatingly they began to intone the prayers for the dead, which at once restored order, the most reverent demeanour being observed by the crowd that filled the building.

Outside, the Swiss guards were drawn up in two lines. The presence of these troops annoyed the people, though they attempted no interference. When the ceremony ended and the *cortège* left for the cemetery, they at once returned to their quarters : they might, indeed, have been supposed a guard of honour. Thus dramatically were the last religious rites of the Church accorded to the great tragic actress.

It was rumoured about, and Louis was by no means displeased that it should be — for there were bitter jealousies and frequent dissensions in the royal family — that the officiating priests were hastily despatched to St. Roch by the king, when informed of the nature of the disturbance ; and that the Swiss guards were sent by the Comte d'Artois, at the instance of the duchess, to enforce obedience to the refusal of the *curé* to allow the body to be brought into the church. Louis was further reported to have said : "All whom the Church has baptised have a right to its prayers when dead."

The pomp and parade with which the royal obsequies of the 21st were performed served but to increase the discontent that prevailed, in the provinces no less than in Paris. The antagonism which existed between the brothers in 1789 seemed to be renewed in 1815, and daily to be increasing. Such liberal views as Louis possessen were systematically opposed and thwarted by the

Comte d'Artois, whom the extreme royalists —
and the king was fully aware of it — would have
greatly preferred to place on the throne.

"No concessions! no concessions!" was the
constant cry of the Pavillon Marsan. But Louis
XVIII., who loved popularity, without, however,
being at much trouble to secure it, rather liked to
be *thought* conceding. He would have nothing
forced upon, or from, him. For, as he said to the
Duc de Richelieu, he was "resolved to be king to
the full extent of the term." But, of his *bon
plaisir* — as in the case of the famous Charter —
he might graciously deign to yield to the wishes
of his loving citizens (subjects they refused to
acknowledge themselves) what would endanger
his throne and interfere with his ease and comfort
longer to refuse.

In short, he and his family, his incompetent
ministry, and Jesuit priesthood, were doing their
best to bring about another revolution. But so
secure did they think themselves that no warnings
availed to awaken them to a sense of danger; and
the thunderclap of the 5th of March, in the guise
of a telegraphic announcement to Paris and Vienna
that "the Man of Elba" had left his island, had
landed in France, and was marching on the capi-
ital, took them all by surprise.

CHAPTER XIII.

AVAILING himself of Sir Neil Campbell's temporary absence from the island, Napoleon left Elba on the 26th of February, 1815, his project being further facilitated by the Princesse Pauline Borghese, who invited the notabilities of the mimic empire to a ball that evening. With Généraux Bertrand, Cambronne, and Drouot, and four hundred grenadiers of the old guard, he embarked in the brig of war *L'Inconstant* — six small vessels, with about five hundred other troops on board, accompanying. The island well cleared, "Grenadiers!" exclaimed Napoleon (they were supposed to be unaware of the object of his expedition), "our destination is France! We are going to march on Paris." "*Vive l'empereur!*" was the exulting response, caught up and repeated with enthusiasm by the Polish lancers and Corsican chasseurs in the small vessels following in the wake of the brig.

The little flotilla, escaping the vigilance of the cruisers, was wafted by favourable breezes towards the coast of France. On the 1st of March Napoleon and his companions landed in the vicinity of Cannes. " The Congress is dissolved!" he exclaimed, as he set his foot on shore. Their first bivouac was in an olive grove, which Napoleon thought a good omen. On the morrow he began his triumphal march towards the capital, and on the 5th, joined by Colonel de la Bédoyère, who with his regiment had marched out to meet him, he entered Grenoble, whose inhabitants threw open the gates of their city and welcomed him with every demonstration of joy.

Thus far had the emperor proceeded when the news of his return reached Paris. The Comte d'Artois, the Duc and Duchesse d'Angoulême, and the coterie of the Pavillon Marsan were assembled in the duchess's almonry. In contemptuous pity they shrugged their shoulders, and laughed derisively when informed that the Corsican, escaped from his gaoler with a band of brigands, had had the insensate presumption again to set his foot on the soil of France. Beyond feeing the Virgin with extra wax candles, they were not disposed to adopt any measures of defence. The people were presumed to be so much overawed by

the rule of the right divine that they might well
be trusted to repulse Bonaparte and his band
should they venture to approach the capital.

The king, however, had the advantage of having
his eyes opened by his *amie intime* to the agitation prevailing in Paris, to which his considerate
friend M. Blacas-d'Aulps would fain have had
them closed, lest the righteous spirit of his sacred
majesty should be inordinately vexed by it.

"I gave you due warning, Sire, you know," said
the fair countess, reproachfully. "I told your
majesty that the Duchesse de Saint-Leu's charades
meant more than mere amusement; that those
generals and colonels were not so assiduous in
their attendance mornings and evenings for the
mere pleasure of rehearsing and acting in them."
Many other signs also she mentioned of secret
intrigues of which she believed she had found the
key; nor did she forget the Krüdener prophecy.

Acting on her advice, Louis immediately convoked the Legislative Chambers, and assembled
the *corps diplomatique.* A decree, published the
next morning, enjoined all governors, commanders, and military men of whatever rank, as well
as all civilians, to lay hands on and arrest the traitor Bonaparte wherever and whenever he should
be met with. The Comte d'Artois, accompanied
by Général Gouvion Saint Cyr, set off, at the
urgent request of the king, to take the command
of the troops at Lyons, where the Duc d'Orléans

and Maréchal Macdonald were to join him.   The
rest of the generals and marshals of the empire who
held commands were also ordered to repair immediately to their posts.

Roused from their apathy, or their pious confidence in the protection of Heaven, by this general
and sudden activity in the state, the Duc and
Duchesse d'Angoulême proceeded to Bordeaux to
stimulate the wavering royalism of the people of
that city and other towns of the Department of
the Drôme.   The Duc de Berry remained in Paris
to play Henri IV. ; frequenting the theatres and
other public places, to provoke by his presence
cries of " *Vive le roi !   Vivent les Bourbons !*" etc.

The proclamation of Maréchal Soult, inveighing
against "the man who had tyrannised over, deso-
lated, and betrayed France ; " the promise of
Maréchal Ney to the king to " bring back the
Corsican ogre fettered, and confined in an iron
cage," apparently did not quite set his majesty's
mind at ease, for he deprived the former of his
post of Minister of War ; thus, at a critical moment, taking a good deal of power out of his
hands.   He probably remembered, too, his own
rash promise to the marshals " to march with
them, should it be needful again to unsheathe the
sword of France," as he complained to the Senate and the ambassadors of his gout, and of the
annoyance it gave him.   He protested, however,
that he did not intend to leave Paris ; but would

wait tranquilly in his palace, and there on his throne face to face confound the usurper, whom he in no manner feared.

Bold words, indicating a dauntless spirit. But it was known that, like his partisans, the king already was quaking in his shoes, or rather in his velvet boots, as nearer and nearer the conquering hero advanced. Vainly it was attempted to deceive the people by false and ridiculous reports in that truthful paper, the *Moniteur*, and the generally veracious royalist journals; for wherever the magic sound of Napoleon's voice again fell on the ears of the troops, and the banished *tricolor* was once more seen waving before them, the white cockade and white banner were speedily trodden under foot; and as this was of daily occurrence, no efforts of the government could long conceal it from the Parisians.

On the 10th, Napoleon entered Lyons in triumph, welcomed by the joyous acclamations of the people, and in spite of Macdonald's order to close the gates against him, which the troops refused to obey. The Comte d'Artois, who nominally commanded, did not enter Lyons, but fled with all speed back to Paris, his escort being a single gendarme to point out the nearest and safest by-roads. Macdonald soon followed. The Duc d'Orléans also decamped without beat of drum, to look after his own private interests, of course, his partisans seeing a chance open to him

in this new revolution.   The emperor was thus
left undisputed master of Lyons and its garrison.
There he remained three days, issuing decrees,
dissolving the Chambers, and convoking the electoral colleges of the empire to a meeting extraordinary of the "Champ de Mai," to take place in
Paris on the 1st of May.   He proposed there to
correct and modify the various constitutions imposed on France since 1789, in order to bring
them more into harmony with the wishes of the
nation.

There, too, the nation was invited to assist at
the coronation of the empress and the King of
Rome.   The emperor did not seem to be aware
that Maria Louisa had renounced her title of
empress, that the imperial arms and cipher were
already effaced from her carriages, and that she
would never, if willing, be permitted to return to
him, unless, perhaps, he could hold France and
defy Europe in arms against him ; and this had
yet to be proved.   Meanwhile, she was by no
means saddened by the existing events of the past
year.   If *les convenances* forbade for the time
being any participation in the unceasing round of
courtly gaieties that chiefly employed the time
and attention of the Congress, yet she was not
doomed to lonely widowhood at Schönbrunn.   At
that pleasant retreat she discussed her affairs *tête-
à-tête* at breakfast with the Emperor Alexander,
entertained a small party of kings and princes at

luncheon, or, with one or two more favoured than the rest, rambled through its shady grounds and gardens.

She is said to have demanded and insisted in a manner quite Napoleonic with reference to the Italian states that were to be assigned to her. But in this she was inspired by Count Neipperg, who had his own views in the matter, and whose influence over her was paramount.

As to the emperor's son, he was not only no longer King of Rome, the poor child was not even Napoleon. The name was taken from him, together with his grand cross of the Legion of Honour. A German name and a German order were substituted for them, and he was removed from the guardianship of his mother, who, indeed, evinced but little affection for him. Thus the too hastily announced coronation of the Champ de Mai was destined never to take place.

When Napoleon left Lyons on the 13th, by what he had abolished and what he had restored, he had effaced with his pen the eleven months of the Restoration. This the government kept profoundly secret, as far as they were able. But to counteract any ill effects it might have, should the news too soon ooze out that by imperial decree the Bourbons were banished, their estates seques-tered, the Swiss regiments, *gardes du corps*, etc., disbanded, the Orders of Saint Louis, Saint Esprit, and Saint Michel annulled, and the

Legion of Honour restored to its former importance, a royal *séance* was announced for the 16th.
The great dignitaries of the kingdom then repaired, with much pomp, to the legislative chamber, where Louis, seated in an armchair placed
on a canopied dais, and surrounded by the princes,
including the Comte d'Artois,— whom all were
surprised to see, and supposed he had gained
some great victory,— read an address, sketched
by himself and revised by the eloquent M. de
Jouy.   In it he formally announced that the
foreign Powers would aid him to expel the "public
enemy" who came again to impose his iron yoke
on the nation and to destroy the constitutional
charter.   "Let us rally around our Charter! Let
it be our sacred standard!" he exclaimed, as if
suddenly inspired.   The whole assembly, catching
as it were the monarch's enthusiasm, arose, and
"*Vive le roi! vive la Charte!*" echoed throughout
the building.

The excitement calmed down, the Comte
d'Artois stepped forward, and, raising his hand
towards heaven, said, in his own and his family's
name :   "We swear by our honour to live and die
faithful to our king, and to the Charter which
assures the welfare of all Frenchmen."

"We swear it!" repeated the princes, raising
their hands and looking upwards.   All who were
present — and the chamber was packed with a
select and selected audience — repeated : "We

swear it!" while the king extended his arms towards his brother, who rushed into them and wept. Then followed mutual embracing, tears of joy, and expressions of admiring wonder at the goodness, the graciousness, the noble words, and the noble conduct of the king. This scene is said to have been fully arranged and rehearsed before it was publicly performed. It produced an abundant crop of epigrams and *chansons*, which was by no means the result intended.

It had been proposed to seduce the grenadiers of the old guard from their persistent allegiance to their emperor by offering those who would swear fidelity to Louis XVIII. the rank of officers, and to the officers themselves letters of nobility. But the project was abandoned when it became known that, on the same day that the moving scene above mentioned took place, Maréchal Ney addressed his troops in a proclamation, telling them that the cause of the Bourbons was lost — lost forever! Two days after, at Auxerre, Ney and his detachment joined the emperor.

There still lingered in Paris a few foreigners and others, whose duty it was to wait until the king gave the order for departure, and who professed to hope or believe that "the usurper's daring enterprise" might even now receive an effectual check before he reached Paris. But at Fontainebleau the people were in a ferment of delight at his approach, and the servants at the Château were busily preparing for his reception.

Generally, the English ladies fled from the capital when the Duchess of Wellington took wing. Hortense, with her two sons, was in Paris, waiting to receive, while prepared to depart, as the chapter of accidents should determine. The Comtesse du Cayla, serenely calm, and unruffled by passing events, was vigilantly watching her own and her royal friend's interests. She is said to have counselled him to remain in France; while M. Blacas-d'Aulps urged departure for England, where, indeed, he was generally expected.

Madame de Staël, whose fierce republicanism had been greatly subdued by the expected payment of her two millions, had waited for the Corsican's discomfiture almost longer than seemed prudent. But besides the expected receipt of the two millions, she was on the eve of marrying her daughter to the Duc de Broglie, which auspicious event was deferred by the dispersion of society and the upset in the government the *contretemps* of Napoleon's return had occasioned. M. Rocca, too, was growing anxious on her account; so go she must. The clique that, for interested reasons, always accompanied her were glad to hear this decision; and that bundle of sentimentality and affectation, Madame Moreau, fearing that something terrible would occur to her for daring to visit Paris, was persuaded to take the road to Coppet also.

Louis grew daily less firm in his resolution to remain in Paris; it became evident that he desired to be persuaded to leave. His hopes had been placed in the prowess of the great soldier Angoulême. They had now faded away, news having arrived that, instead of gaining great victories, he had capitulated, had been detained as a hostage; afterwards was released by Napoleon's order, and, on delivering up a portion of the crown diamonds he had with him, had embarked for Spain. But what had become of the duchess? With a nodding plume of feathers in her hat, she was playing the heroine in the South. Whatever royalists Bordeaux contained gathered around her, of course. But she had not the gift of graciousness, the fascination of manner, or the tact needed to win converts, and especially when it was desired to convert old soldiers of the empire into royalists. The commandant was utterly powerless to restrain them from joining Général Clausel, then marching into Bordeaux with his volunteers, the *tricolor* flying, and shouting "*Vive l'empereur!*" She, however, gave orders very imperiously to arrest both them and the general, and when the commandant informed her respectfully that he could not obey her, "I will deprive you of your commission!" she exclaimed. "Madame," he replied, "I received my commission from the king. If I fail in my duty it is for his majesty, not you, to withdraw it. Bloodshed and civil war would be the result of attempting obedience to your commands."

Already on the fortress the *tricolor* had displaced the white banner, and the garrison were exulting over the return of their emperor. The haughty duchess was assailed with cries of "*À bas les Bourbons ! à bas les plumes !*" Her presence seemed to exasperate the people almost as much as the troops. She was, therefore, prevailed on to leave Bordeaux ; and on that same evening, accompanied by the mayor and a few royalists, she hastily embarked at Pouillon for Spain, whence she afterwards proceeded to London.

Napoleon, meanwhile, has reached Fontainebleau. The news causes a panic at the Tuileries, and a general *sauve qui peut* among the old emigrants and pure royalists. "The king's philosophy," wrote M. de Jaucourt to Talleyrand, "points to Hartwell." But while hesitating which road he will take — for his fear of being made prisoner proves stronger than his sense of dignity — the coffers of the state are emptied for his use, and that portion of the crown jewels which the Duc and Duchesse d'Angoulême had not taken away are packed up in his travelling-carriage.

At near midnight on the 19th, Louis, with some difficulty, was removed from his bed to begin his journey. His gout troubled him greatly, and on such occasions he was accustomed to give way to violent outbursts of temper, and, instead of em-

bellishing his discourse with Latin quotations as
at other times, to substitute profane oaths, which
much shocked the ears polite compelled to hear
them. That his tantrums, under the circumstances, should on this journey exceed all bounds,
is not to be wondered at ; but doubtless they were
a sore trial even to the calmly enduring Père
Élisée, who accompanied his royal patient, as well
as to the .officer of the *gardes du corps* who was
his sole escort. However, the secret flitting was
safely accomplished, and on arriving at Lille, the
fair countess, who had preceded him, was at hand
to receive and console her sovereign, and to report
all that was going on amongst friends and foes of
the monarchy.

But stealthily as the king had left the Tuileries,
vigilant watchers, on the *qui vive* to surprise every
movement in the palace, were so well aware of it
that a messenger was on the road to Fontainebleau
bearing the news before the royal traveller was
even comfortably seated, much less fairly out of
Paris. It was a busy night in the capital; private
carriages and public vehicles were traversing it in
all directions, for the various members of the government and household were preparing to follow
their royal master, and to depart before sleeping
Paris awoke on the morning of the 20th.

The Château of the Tuileries was deserted,
the government offices and ministerial residences
nearly so, when Général de La Valette, Director

of the Posts under the empire, boldly reinstated himself, and despatched to Lyons and other chief towns of France the departure of the " Comte de Lille " from Paris and the expected arrival of the emperor.

The 20th of March was a day of much expectation and anxiety in Paris. Some writers have said that the return of the great captain was dreaded by all but the soldiery. Others equally trustworthy and more disinterested have declared that the Parisians of all classes vied with each other in the enthusiastic expression of their admiration of, and devotion to him. The departure of the Bourbons, with their priests and their processions, their right divine to govern wrong, and their Jesuitical Charter, was indeed something to rejoice over. For twenty-four hours after their flight Paris was left in the power of the people — no police, no constituted authority of any kind; yet never had the capital been more peaceful or the populace more orderly.

All day long the country people, and, more numerously, the dwellers in the outskirts, were bringing in baskets full of violets. The garden in front of the Tuileries was literally covered with these floral offerings, emblems of the event of the day, their fragrant odour perfuming the palace and surrounding atmosphere. The *tricolor* floated again on the Tuileries and the Vendôme column, Général Exelmans having hoisted them early in the afternoon amid general enthusiasm, the white banner descending to the cry of "*À bas les Bourbons!*"

Towards evening, a large party, military and civilian, some of them old companions in arms, rode out as far as Corbeil to meet the emperor and welcome him. An immense crowd, as eager again to see him as when in former days he returned from a successful campaign, also assembled around the approaches of the palace.

But it is near nine o'clock. The hero himself must be approaching; for through the thickening gloom of night the lurid light of torches, gleaming at intervals on the casques and lances of the *avant - garde*, is visible. Presently the tramp of horses' feet is heard, louder still and nearer. It is the company of Polish lancers. Immediately they are surrounded and eagerly questioned.

"He is coming, friends!" they reply. He is close at hand — near, quite near. *Vive l'empereur!* A hearty response is returned by the assembled thousands, as the 4th division of hussars ride up and join in the exulting cry. The people seem frantic, rushing hither and thither, embracing each other, now weeping with excess of joy, now full of laughter and mutual congratulations.

A second company of torch-bearers advances, riding on each side of a carriage drawn by six horses (one of the imperial equipages found in the

magazines of Villejuif, and with arms and cipher
not yet effaced).   Rapidly it rolls on until it enters the courtyard of the Tuileries.   There the
multitude take eager possession of it.   The door
is thrown open, and Napoleon, much moved (and
such a scene and such a reception might well
move the sternest and most self-possessed), when
about to alight, is prevented by the eager rush of
the people, and is literally carried by them into
the palace and to the top of the grand staircase.
There so closely do they press around him that he
gasps out, "Gentlemen, you stifle me!"

In the grand *salon* he at last breathes freely.
There, Hortense, with a few ladies, M. de Monta-
livet, and a numerous company of devoted adherents, are assembled heartily to greet him.

The battalion of Elba, those faithful grenadiers
of the old guard who had shared the exile of their
emperor and escorted him on his return, arrived
later and bivouacked that night on the Place de
Carrousel.   They were weary and footsore after
their march of 250 leagues.   Many, being shoe-
less, had bandaged their bleeding feet.   Their
uniforms, too, were torn and travel-soiled.   But a
joyous smile lighted up their sunburnt features,
and when their emperor appeared next day on the
Place to pass them in review, to thank them for
having so well done their duty, and for their attachment and fidelity to him, these weather-beaten
veterans presented both an interesting and pic-

turesque *ensemble*.   Cries of " *Vive la vieille garde! Vive l'empereur!*" rent the air, the old soldiers, as was their due, fully sharing the enthusiasm of the ovation accorded by the people to their general.

CHAPTER XIV.

Departures and Arrivals. — A Familiar Process. — "A Subjéct
of Raillery." — What Means Shall He Choose? — A Famous
Philippic. — A Discreet and Devoted Friend. — The Love-
lorn Swain's Return. — From Lille to Ghent. — King of Kings.
— His Serene Highness in London. — "*Le Petit Guizot.*" —
The Lover a Councillor of State. — A New Constitution.
— Approved by Madame de Staël. — The Captious Lover. —
Honour Avenged.

HE *Journal des Débats*, already trans-
formed into the *Journal de l'Empire*,
announced, as follows, in its issue of
the 21st, the change that had taken place in the
ruling powers of France : " His majesty the king,
with the princes of his family, left his palace of
the Tuileries, early on the morning of the 20th,
for Lille."

" His majesty the Emperor Napoleon arrived at
his palace of the Tuileries from Fontainebleau at
nine on the evening of the 20th."

Following the example of their sovereign, some
few royalists had affected to cast fear to the winds
when they heard of the " Corsican's escape." But
on becoming unmistakably aware that the dauntless
Louis had fled, like him they were in a terrible
state of alarm lest they should fall into the Corsi-

can's clutches. Immediately there was a frantic demand for post-horses. But both the outgoing and the incoming head of the state had ordered the seizure of all that were available; so that, generally, laggards who felt themselves in any way compromised had to find their way out of Paris as best they could, or to seek some safe shelter within it wherein to hide their diminished heads.

On the whole, however, there was nothing very terrible to fear. Such danger as there was, except in a few — and very few — instances, might still be avoided by a process with which many were already familiar, that of adroitly turning their coats. The political writer M. de Jouy,* who usually revised the speeches which Louis XVIII. prepared for himself, put in a few finishing touches, and corrected quotations, — Louis's memory having become a little hazy, — had turned his coat a twelvemonth ago, and was about to *re*-turn it, fully intending to turn it again if need there should be. And again, and still again, he was destined to do so, each time revising his writings, which were popular, to bring them into harmony more or less with his change of sentiments and opinions.

An order to reside at a distance of forty leagues from the capital was the worst that fate seemed to have in store for the most loyal of

* Author of " *L'hermite de la chaussée d' Antin*," etc.

Louis's adherents.   One, however, there was who,
without laying claim to much loyalty, had really
gone out of his way grossly to insult the emperor
in an article published in the *Journal des Débats*
on the eve of his return to Paris.   This was
Benjamin Constant.   As already stated, he was
passionately, madly, in love with Madame Récamier; and although this mad love had endured
near a twelvemonth, the fervour of his unrequited
passion seems rather to have increased than
abated.   "You make my anguish," he wrote, "a
subject of raillery." . If so, it must have been
either in conversation with him, or in writing, of
which she was very sparing; for there seems to
have been no confidant on either side of the state
of things between them.

Driven to despair, this most romantic of mid-
dle-aged lovers writes: "You are both heaven and
God to me.   When heaven is closed, and God
repulses, I feel that hell has seized me.   All that
is good or gentle in my nature revives or dies at
your bidding.   You are the tutelary genius, or
the exterminating angel, at your choice."   But
Madame Récamier accepts neither alternative;
and Constant, unable to inspire her with any
responsive feeling, will at least, as he writes,
wring from her coldness pity — pity for the man
whose career she has destroyed, and who has
sought death as the only means of extinguishing
his love.   Thus while all Paris was in a state of

Benjamin Constant.
Photo-etching after the painting by Guibert.

stupor and expectation, " Benjamin Constant — a
man," says M. de Loménie, " of forty-eight years,
a *blasé* man of the world, but with a heart all
flame — was occupied with one thought only,"
that of seeking, in the general overthrow about to
take place, some means of making himself pitied
by the woman he loved.

What means shall he choose, or will fate or
fortune throw in his way ? Shall he fight for the
Bourbons at the barriers ? But it does not appear
that he was likely to distinguish himself and subdue a lady's heart as a fighting hero. Besides,
there was nothing singular in it ; there would be
no lack of younger, if not braver, men, if fighting
there should be, to unsheathe the sword and die
for the Bourbons. The weapon he best could
wield was the pen, and with it, while others held
back, he would advance and deal a blow so heavy
on the usurper then marching on Paris, that it
should recoil on himself in the form of a sentence
of banishment or death. Thus the rejected lover
would become a being so essentially interesting
that the cruel fair one might even feel a slight
pang of remorse when she learned his fate, but
could not fail to drop a tear of pity to the memory
of the lover she had slighted.

On the 19th of March, Louis XVIII. being
then at the Tuileries, this famous philippic, signed
in full, appears. Napoleon is addressed as the
" man stained with blood, as a fallen tyrant pur-

sued by the maledictions of the universe; as
Attila, as Genghis Khan — his tyranny even more
terrible than theirs, because the resources of
civilisation are at his disposal." After much
more of the same kind of bitter invective, he
concludes in a defiant tone expressive of his
intention neither to fly from the consequences
of his act nor to stammer out words of degradation to purchase a life of shame.

His friends are amazed at his audacity. They
urge him to leave Paris while yet opportunity is
left to do so. He will not. Is not Madame
Récamier in Paris? That of course he could
whisper only to himself, but it suffices to bear
him up against the worst that could happen. She
had declined accompanying Madame de Staël to
Coppet, and refused at the eleventh hour to allow
Auguste de Staël to escort her thither. Constant
had approved that decision, because he was no
longer a welcome guest there himself, his present
relations with the châtelaine of Coppet being of
a very different character from those of former
days.

He had, however, very earnestly entreated the
idol of his heart to place herself beyond the reach
of Napoleon's displeasure by going to Berlin.
That so discreet and devoted a friend as himself
should see her there in safety was, he said, quite
a matter of course, and could not possibly give
any occasion for scandal. Why, he argued, by

her presence in Paris, should she draw Napoleon's
attention, not only on herself, but on M. Récamier, whose banking business might be disadvan-
tageously affected by it? But Madame Récamier
was deaf to his entreaties, and refused to believe
that she incurred any danger. She wisely considered that, under the changed aspect of political
affairs, matters more important than waging war
on her would demand the emperor's attention.

While M. Constant is waiting to be arrested
and shot, his friends are pressing him to depart;
and at last, Général de La Fayette prevails on
him to accept a temporary shelter offered by the
American minister. On the 23d they have persuaded him to set out for Nantes that he may
reach the coast and embark. In dreadful dudg-
eon he departs. His friends, not possessing the
key to the enigma, think that he at last has
become alarmed at his own temerity. Arrived
at Nantes the love-lorn swain finds absence from
the beloved object insupportable. The separation,
he reflects, may be for years, or it may be forever! Horrid thought! it drives him to desperation; so he orders post-horses and at once sets
out on his return.

On the 27th he is again in Paris. Well may
his friends think that there is a touch of madness in him, and give him up in despair to be
imprisoned or shot, as that seems to be his will.
He, however, walks about Paris, shows himself

very openly, and to his mortification no notice whatever is taken of him by the police; the object of his invective seems to be as impervious to his attacks as the marble heart of Madame Récamier to his love. True that Genghis Khan is much occupied at present. Yet the government appears to be going on as if no interruption had occurred, everything and everybody connected with it having fallen quite naturally into their places again.

Meanwhile, Louis, for the second time, has fled in a panic. Cries of "*À bas les Bourbons!*" meet his ear at Lille, and the hated *tricolor* floats before his eyes on the fortress. The garrison of Lille, he discovers, is by no means well disposed towards him, but very well inclined to make him prisoner. He therefore beats a hasty retreat during the night of the 23d, and arrives at Ghent on the 24th, all fume and fury, but with some slight relief to his gout. A decree disbanding the army, and another inciting the people generally to refuse payment of the imposts, were left behind him to be proclaimed at Lille; but both were disregarded.

The Comte d'Artois and Duc de Berry, who had been looking up recruits for the royal cause, arrived at Lille, followed by a party of volunteers, soon after Louis's departure. A scowling reception awaited them, both from the military and the civilians; consequently they made no attempt to maintain themselves there, but, following the king's example, crossed the frontier, and Belgium then became the rendezvous of a second emigration.

Soon they were joined by the Duc d'Angoulême, who, with his friends the Ducs de Polignac, Lévis, Guiche-d'Escars, and Damas, reached Ghent by way of Calais. Thither, too, hastened MM. de Châteaubriand, Beugnot, Baron Louis, and others, the last to arrive being M. de Talleyrand, from Vienna. At Ghent, Louis, who under all the changes and chances of fortune thought himself king of kings, as regarded earthly monarchs, "a king everywhere, as God is God everywhere, — in a manger or a temple, on an altar of clay or of gold," * — revived in miniature the court of Versailles, with the obsolete etiquette of the old *régime* strictly observed. And there the *amie intime*, or *maîtresse-en-titre*, the intriguing Comtesse du Cayla, served as the medium of communication between the intriguers of Paris and his majesty the King of Ghent.

None was there to thwart her influence, which — though making use of it when it served their purposes — the Comte d'Artois and Duchesse d'Angoulême were accustomed to do. But the duchess, her chief opponent, was in London, and, at the king's desire, vigilantly watching the manœuvres of the Duc d'Orléans. He had passed over to England with his family on the emperor's

* *Mémoires d'outre-tombe.*

arrival at Fontainebleau. Immediately, and before the final dispersion of the Congress, he forwarded two memorials to Vienna, setting forth the causes of the overthrow of the Bourbons in 1792 and 1815. When Louis XVIII. was informed of this fact by M. de Talleyrand, his indignation was extreme, and so furiously expressed that the skill of the Père Élisée scarcely sufficed to avert fatal consequences. " The duchess was therefore deputed to counteract by every possible means the influence his serene highness was supposed to exert over the mind of the prince regent, who was known to take much interest in the son of the former companion of his infamous orgies." *

At Ghent, too, was established the famous " Journal, whose chief object was to circulate in the provinces, in opposition to the statements of the *Moniteur de Paris*, a falsified account of what the ' usurper and his myrmidons ' were doing in Paris, and to inculcate the dogma of the right divine of kings." The principal contributors to the *Moniteur· de Gand* were MM. de Châteaubriand and Guizot. The latter, who was editor of the journal, had found his way to Ghent and returned to his allegiance only after his dismissal by Carnot from the office he had held under the Abbé Montesquiou, but, at his earnest solicitation, had been retained — provisionally only

* *Mémoires de la famille d'Orléans.*

— when the government changed hands. Louis XVIII. said he had a sort of affection for *"le petit Guizot,"* as he had never known a royalist who could so thoroughly disguise himself as a liberal.

But while Louis was waiting at Ghent the arrival of the allies to reconquer France for him, — his princely and priestly *entourage*, meanwhile, solely occupied in the business of devotion and the fabrication of reports whose aim was to raise and extend the prestige of royalty, — Napoleon was diligently pursuing the path he at first marked out for himself. The promises made at the Restoration, but forgotten as soon as made, Napoleon was applying himself to fulfil. The man, too, who had said, "The author of the most tyrannical of constitutions now talks of liberty. What liberty can he insure to us? He promises peace, and his name alone is a signal for war. His triumph would be but the beginning of a mortal combat against the civilised world. He has then nothing to claim, nothing to offer!" — this man had now rallied to the imperial standard.

Instead of arresting Benjamin Constant, Napoleon — who well knew the character of the man he had to deal with, knew his habits and the needs of his existence — expressed a wish to converse with him, through those partisans of liberalism whom the promised reforms had drawn around him. This wish was made known to his antago-

nist.   An interview was appointed, and Constant
prevailed on by his friends to attend.   The result
was the natural one.   The weaker will succumbed
to the stronger.   That indefinable fascination,
which Prince Metternich and others have spoken
of as existing in Napoleon's smile and conversation, had their usual effect, and Constant was
convinced, by the irresistible arguments brought
to bear on him, of the justice of the emperor's
views.   Believing, too, in the thoroughness of
his determination to abjure henceforth the oppressive principles of the empire, and openly to
adopt the liberal ideas of the constitutional party,
he accepted the post of Councillor of State.

The emperor, however, did not profess to regard
those ideas in a more favourable light than formerly.   He frankly acknowledged that he perceived he could no longer govern France by any
other; therefore he adopted them.   " He had
given the nation, he said, glory and prosperity;
in future he would give her prosperity and peace
— if his enemies would let him."   From the pen
of the new Councillor of State he then requested
the project of a new constitution.

A new constitution for France !   What a task !
Arduous indeed in peaceful times, even for a man
with thoughts and feelings wholly absorbed by
anxious desire to promote the welfare and the
best interests of his country.   How then shall he
accomplish the task whose heart is ravaged by the

pangs of love so distracting that it sends him forth
to loiter in the street near his lady-love's dwelling,
that perchance he may snatch a glimpse of her
shadow as she crosses her apartment? Maybe he
has called on her, and been told that "*Madame
n'est pas visible.*" He then lingers awhile on the
enchanted spot, — perhaps he will have the felicity
of seeing her go out or go in,— and has for his
pains but the further mortification and anguish to
see a more favoured friend admitted, or a more
discreet one, who will be content to adore and to
receive in return her sympathy and friendship
without wearying her with the language of love.

But the councillor must begin his task, and it is
she who must inspire him. He pens an epistle ;
tells her of his interview. He dares not tell her
what passed ; but he knows she is prudent — and
if she is curious, and will receive him for half an
hour, and for that brief space admit no other visitor, she may hear from him, he says, much that is
interesting. The lady is curious,— who among
womankind is not ? — therefore graciously grants
his request. Two or three similar interviews follow, which help him to get triumphantly through
his task.

"*L'Acte additionnel*" appears to have met with
the full approval of Madame de Staël. Writing
from Coppet to Joseph Bonaparte, she says : " The
additional articles are all that is needed for France ;
nothing but what is needed, and no more than is

needed. Your brother's return is marvellous, it surpasses imagination." The fact of the "*Acte additionnel*" having been drawn up by Benjamin Constant may have in some measure influenced her judgment. She had reproached him before she left Paris with wasting his time and talents. "By his very strange conduct," she said, "he would soon lose all his friends. She herself took no further interest in him ; and if it was love that had brought him to that pitiable condition, who-ever might be the object of that love, she would never care anything for him." "Too true, alas !" he exclaimed, poor fellow, when he repeated this to Madame Récamier, who had the cruelty to laugh. A slight mitigation of severity towards him now that he is Councillor of State gains him readmission to Madame Récamier's evening receptions after the opera. But he can so little command his feelings that he betrays some annoyance, fancying that she receives some other of her train of adorers more cordially, or smiles on him more graciously than on himself.

With Baron Montlosier he comes to such high words in her *salon* on the subject of feudal rights that a duel is the consequence. Madame Réca-mier is naturally anxious. A political quarrel in her *salon* with such a result is likely to compromise her at a time when so much agitation prevails respecting public affairs. She would also be glad that her friends should quietly make up their dis-

pute. This, they urge, would be everlasting disgrace to both of them. Blood must be shed. But
in the event of the baron killing his adversary or
his adversary killing him, a letter is written by M.
Constant to be delivered to Napoleon, to assure
him that Madame Récamier, whose prudence and
moderate political opinions are well known, was in
no way connected with the duel.

The meeting takes place in the Bois de Boulogne. A wound in the sword hand at once dis-
ables the baron and puts an end to the duel. But
the honour of both is avenged. The reconciliation
of the combatants follows as a matter of course,
this happy termination of their quarrel allowing
the councillor to appear in his place at the grand
ceremony of the " Champ de Mai," to take place
on the first of June.

CHAPTER XV.

HE ceremony of the "Champ de Mai,"
which the electoral colleges were convoked to attend in Paris, did not take
place till the 1st of June. The occurrence of un-
foreseen circumstances, tending to overthrow the
emperor's plans and to endanger the stability of
the throne so lately reconquered, had caused this
delay. Nevertheless, his own calmness and confidence, together with that almost miraculous resus-
citation, immediately following his appearance, of
the usual orderly routine of the business of government and the service of the palace, inspired
those about him with hope and courage.

Since his return he had diligently sought to
regain and augment his popularity among the
people, who, as experience had taught him, were

in fact his firmest supporters. The manufactories, the workrooms, the colleges, the public establishments, all in their turn were visited by him; and he had used these opportunities to distribute crosses, to confer pensions, and to speak words of encouragement wherever merit or promise of excellence seemed to deserve such recognition. He went through various parts of the capital also, sometimes on foot, at others on horseback or in a carriage, showing himself everywhere, and everywhere his presence was the signal for an enthusiastic ovation.

The "*Acte additionnel,*" the equivalent of a new constitution, after much discussion and some opposition, was now finally agreed to as embodying the reforms needed by France. It remained that it should be publicly accepted both by the emperor and by the representatives of the nation. Though the manner of doing this was cavilled at by many as theatrical, as indeed all such public ceremonies, pageants, processions, etc., more or less necessarily must be, yet the accounts of disinterested eye-witnesses declare that the grand spectacle of the 1st of June in the Champ de Mars was both solemn and impressive.

Considering the wholesale slaughter of the people which had occurred in France since 1790, probably few, if any, among the vast crowd assembled on the present occasion — outnumbering far that of the former one — took part in the *fête* of the Federation. Généraux de La Fayette and Carnot, Cambacérès and Fouché, with one or two others, and perhaps the emperor himself, would be almost the only persons who had witnessed it. Yet one can readily imagine that the *fête* of the 1st of June, 1815, suggested to many minds that of the 14th of July, 1790 — even to the possibility of sinister results following it.

Mass was celebrated in the Champ de Mars, as at the Federal *fête*, to impart more solemnity to the ceremony. An unwilling emperor was present (he regretted as premature the promise of a " Champ de Mai," made in a moment of elation at Lyons), as there was an unwilling king at the July *fête*, and for the same purpose — to inaugurate a new era of liberty in France, and to bind themselves by oath to faithfully administer the provisions of the new constitution. The multitude in their turn, after the delegates, swore also to be bound by them, and, pressing around towards the altar and throne, repeated in chorus, "*Nous le jurons.*" Volleys of artillery now, as then, announced that the compact between the sovereign and the people was completed, while the air rang with acclamations, and, at the later scene, with reiterated cries of " *Vive l'empereur! Vive la nation!* " — the people as they dispersed singing the Marseillaise, which had not been heard in Paris since the revolution.

Louis XVI. was accompanied by the haughty

and indignant Marie Antoinette and her son ; and it was part of the Lyons programme that an Austrian princess and her son should grace the present scene. If, as announced, there had been the novel spectacle of an empress and a King of Rome to crown in the presence of the people, the ceremony would have been grander and more imposing. The emperor's costume, too, probably prepared for that event, would have been more appropriate. It consisted of a gold-embroidered violet velvet mantle of state, crimson velvet tunic, a velvet toque and white plume, white satin vest and breeches, white satin shoes with diamond buckles ; grand cross of the Legion of Honour in diamonds and rubies, and diamond-hilted sword.

Perhaps, as he then appeared as a legislator, his usual uniform of the chasseurs and his three-cornered hat would have formed too striking a contrast with his brothers' violet mantles of state, embroidered with golden bees, and with the robes of office of the grand dignitaries of his household ; all of whom were grouped around him, with the chiefs of the various departments of government. Yet had he worn a general's uniform, the great soldier *par excellence* would have shown to greater advantage. He had not yet beaten his sword into a ploughshare, but was diligently preparing for war, and about to lead forth his troops to meet Europe in arms against him ; about to fight a battle, on the result of which depended his own and the nation's destiny; and this "Champ de Mai" might well be, as it proved to be, and many had a presentiment that it was so, his public and final farewell to the French people.

Maria Louisa had now an opportunity afforded her of playing a striking part in the closing scene of Napoleon's career. She has been reproached with want of energy at this critical period, but she was wanting much more in inclination to rejoin her husband. He certainly had not failed in his duty towards her or her child; but she turned her back on and abandoned him, as readily as any of those traitorous turncoats on whom he had lavished favours and fortune.

Her household was now fully reappointed, as was also that of the King of Rome. But few posts in them had been — as in a more settled state of things they would have been — sought for with any eagerness. The ladies nominated to them (two or three of whom declined the proffered honour) accepted the favour the emperor considered he conferred on them with the almost certain conviction that they would prove merely nominal appointments, and be held but for a very short time. Yet they continued to wear their violets, as did the wives of all the imperialists who again were in office. But as the season of violets was passing away, artificial flowers took the place of the natural ones, and thus may be said to have represented the waning feeling of the wearers ; if not that of fidelity, at all events of the hope of any durable return of the former glory and splendour of the empire.

Hortense, though at first rather harshly re-proached by Napoleon, her acceptance of the title of Duchesse de Saint-Leu from Louis XVIII. being a rankling thorn in the flesh to him, yet did the honours of the imperial court, *en attendant* the possible arrival of Maria Louisa — no very burden-some office, it being little more than a sinecure at that period of general anxiety and restless expectation.

But Napoleon was even more indignant at the conduct of Joséphine in holding communication with the Bourbons. "Those," he said, — and in this remark he included Hortense, — "who have shared in the prosperity of a family should be willing to share in its adversity." He, however, forgave Hortense. But "he could find," he said, "no excuse for Joséphine." Her conduct, he declared, "cut him to the heart."

"Your name was the last word on her dying lips," murmured the weeping Hortense.

"She should have respected it," he replied, coldly.

Had Joséphine been living he would doubtless have bitterly upbraided her for so cordially receiv-ing Alexander and other opponents of the empire, and for her want of self-respect in asking permis-sion of Louis XVIII. to retain her title of empress.

"It was an ineffaceable title," he said, "beyond the power of any temporal sovereign to annul or to confirm, having been conferred by the Pope himself." Pius VII. appears to have regarded it in the same light, as he upheld Napoleon's title of Emperor of France, declaring it impossible for him to annul it, and recognising him as having been legitimately a reigning sovereign, against the absurd pretension of Louis XVIII. to blot out the great soldier's name from the page of history and the roll of kings, to write in its place his own inglorious one.

It has been asserted that a secret negotiation, conducted by Prince Metternich, was pending between Napoleon and the Austrian emperor, while the former was still on his way to the capital. It was begun at Lyons — the enthusiasm of his reception there, his previous success, and the panic that had seized Louis and his government, leaving no doubt of the enterprise triumphantly terminating in Paris. Napoleon's object was to detach Francis II. from the alliance against him by proposing to abdicate in favour of the King of Rome and the regency of Maria Louisa. It was therefore that he announced their coronation so confidently. He was afterwards, at a date not specified, to abdicate, solemnly and publicly, the ceremony on that occasion to be grand and imposing as the public coronation had been.

That this negotiation came suddenly to an end is said to have been owing to the precipitancy with which King Joachim of Naples withdrew from the coalition and turned his arms against Austria. His base abandonment of Napoleon after the battle of Leipzig had been of immense advantage to the allies, while it greatly increased the emperor's difficulties. His position, however, was not so desperate but that the campaign of 1814, in all probability, would have ended favourably for the French, had not Murat followed Bernadotte's example and joined the enemy.

In the following year Murat again is fated to aid in the downfall of his chief, and at the same time to accelerate his own. But now it is his impetuous ardour to serve him that works the mischief. No sooner is he aware of the success attending Napoleon's daring enterprise, than, believing him to be again the master of Europe, he seeks to convince him of his desire to atone for the past, and that he has been more unfortunate than culpable. But he is not quite disinterested; for the allies, having no further need of him, are seeking a pretext for expelling him from Naples and replacing Ferdinand on his throne.

Assured of this, he at once openly declares for the emperor. At the same time he proclaims the independence of Italy, signing his proclamations as before his defection, " Joachim Napoleon," and calls on the Italian states to fight with him for

freedom — whether from the rule of Austria or
France, or both, does not appear. Austria makes
overtures to him, for Prince Metternich would
willingly serve Joachim for the fair Queen Caroline's sake, and once more, with England, promises him the retention of his kingdom. "Too
late! too late!" replies the impetuous Murat;
"Italy asks for freedom, and freedom she shall
have!"

On the 15th of March, with his 40,000 Neapolitans, he sets out to free Italy, and for a time
carries all before him. The superb King Joachim,
in satin doublet, embroidered mantle, and flowing white plumes, flourishing his riding whip or
brandishing his sword, is welcomed with enthusiasm. He asks permission of the Pope to pass
through Rome. His holiness refuses, and Joachim
passes without it. Bologna received him with
joyous acclamations, and the independence of
Italy is being rapidly accomplished when the
Austrian troops appear in full force and check
the further advance of King Joachim. The rivalry
and jealousy existing amongst the Italian states,
and the general dislike with which the Neapolitans
are regarded by the rest of Italy, complete the
failure of his chivalrous expedition. Several
battles, however, ensue. Joachim's courage and
daring are unfailing; but with his ever decreasing
army he is constantly beaten, and compelled to
fight while retreating, for he is hotly pursued;

Caroline Bonaparte.
Photo-etching after the engraving by Hopwood.

but though recklessly risking his life, and courting death, as it were, as the bullets fly thickly around him, he yet remains wholly unharmed.

Eventually he returns to Naples, and enters his capital *incognito* on the evening of the 18th of May. " Dear Caroline," he exclaims, embracing his wife, " all is lost to me but life; that I have sought to lose, and that alone is spared to me." On the evening of the 19th Murat bids farewell to his wife and children, and leaves Naples for the Isle of Ischia, where he is to embark for France. His few remaining troops are left under the command of General Casa-Lanza, who capitulates on the 20th; and the Austrians are to enter on the 22d.

The queen — Caroline Bonaparte — displayed courage worthy of a sister of Napoleon under these very trying circumstances. She proposed to remain alone at Naples until the 22d, to prevent the city from being pillaged. The palace was lighted up as usual on the 21st, that the crowd of lazzaroni, waiting but the signal to commit every kind of depredation, might be deterred from attacking it ; while the national guard, who obeyed her orders, were stationed as she directed. But the English commodore was in the bay, and threatened to bombard the city if it did not surrender to him. Prince Cariati, by the queen's direction, went immediately on board the commodore's ship *Tremendous ;* and it was arranged, on certain conditions which she assented to, that the queen, her children and suite, and the effects belonging to her, should be received on board and conveyed to some French port of the Mediterranean.

Her departure, however, was suspended by order of the Austrian general, when Admiral Lord Exmouth entered the Bay of Naples. He declared that Commodore Campbell had exceeded his powers, that there must be another capitulation, and the queen be transferred from the protection of England to that of Austria. She and her family were then conveyed to Trieste, whence they were transferred to Prague, and finally to Gratz, where, as Countess Lipano, the ex-queen of Naples was to reside, instead of joining her husband, as had been arranged, in the vicinity of Toulon.

Murat landed in France on the 25th of May, on the same spot where Napoleon, little more than two months before, had disembarked. Immediately he despatched a courier with a letter to his friend Fouché, begging him to announce his arrival in France to the emperor, and his earnest desire to employ his sword in the defence of his country. Fouché, who was then intriguing on all sides, had just before said of Napoleon himself, and to a member of his household: "He is not the man we wanted; but as he has come back to us, and cannot be removed like a pawn on a chess-board, we will see what we can do to keep him."

He, however, did not care to grieve Murat, for whom he seems to have felt some regard, by reporting the emperor's answer, which was to the effect that "the patriotic fervour of the French army was so great and so real that he dared not, had he even desired it, place any of his troops under the command of a man whose treachery to France so filled them with horror that they would refuse to be led by him." Fouché therefore simply bade him wait patiently until Napoleon should acquaint him with his intentions. Already disquieted by the non-arrival of his family at Toulon, and ignorant of the cause of it, Fouché's reply was torture to the impetuous Murat, who knew that Napoleon was preparing with the utmost activity to encounter his foes. For the war was declared by the allies to be undertaken solely against him personally.

To thrust once more an incompetent ruler on an unwilling nation was of course its real object. But even those upholders of the right divine thought it scarcely a sufficient motive to avow for Europe a second time appearing in arms. Had Napoleon been able to take Murat to Belgium with him (as he said when speaking of him at Ste. Helena), there were moments on the fatal 18th when the dauntless intrepidity of that brave officer, charging at the head of his cavalry, would have broken the English squares and won the battle. But fate had decreed otherwise. The battle, considering the disparity of numbers, was to the strong. Yet it has been asserted that the true victors at Waterloo were the Prince de Benevento and the Duc d'Otranto — otherwise, the arch-intriguers Talleyrand and Fouché.

However, the celerity with which the emperor prepared to go forth once more to combat the European hosts — and everything had to be prepared — was regarded as wonderful. The army was wholly reorganised; and with amazing activity he collected his dispersed battalions, formed and drilled new ones, and provided ammunition and other military stores to replace those abundant supplies which in the preceding year the allies had appropriated, and which were probably now used for the equipment of the armies brought against him.

Had he found his fortresses and arsenals as he left them he would have driven the Bourbons and their priestly retinue out of France at once. For the feeling of the nation was doubtless with him, its martial spirit, as subsequent events proved, being more in harmony with military rule than with the perpetual tinkling and tolling of bells, an army of priests, the worship of saints and relics, frequent penances, and the constant succession of ecclesiastical processions — such being the condition to which the Comte d'Artois, his son, and daughter-in-law were urgent in their endeavours to reduce fair France.

The opening of the campaign of 1815 was announced to the French troops in language very similar to Nelson's address to his men at Trafalgar, "England expects that every man will this day do his duty!" On the part of Napoleon it was: "For every Frenchman who has heart and courage, the moment is arrived to conquer or perish." Three Frenchmen, says Lacroix, at once gave proof that they possessed neither, by deserting to the enemy, to whom, as far as they knew the emperor's plans, they revealed them. These contemptible traitors were Général Bourmont and Colonels Clouet and Villoutrays. Fouché, too, was informed of them by Général Davoust, and they were made known to Field Marshal Wellington by the former, a woman in his confidence conveying them to the British lines.

These acts of treachery at the very outset of the campaign would not of course have sufficed to give victory to the allies; but it was because of them that the duke was designated by the French " *Le héros par hasard,*" and that Napoleon's project of surprising the two armies, and placing himself in the space that Wellington and Blücher had left between them, was altogether frustrated. It is not of course in these pages that any detailed account of the great and decisive battle of Waterloo will be looked for — a battle in which, from all authentic accounts, treachery strove to thwart the plans of the great captain, to confuse and dispirit the chiefs, and, though it could not stifle, to check the enthusiasm of the troops.

Napoleon's soldiers entered the Belgian territory in three columns at break of day on the 15th of June, singing the Marseillaise. A hundred and one guns announcing the first success — the victory of Fleurus or Ligny — raised the hopes of his partisans. But the slaughter was so great that the so-called victory was a loss to the French rather than a gain. Yet Blücher was near falling into their hands. His horse, being wounded by a ball, rushed madly onward till, strength failing him, he fell dead, bringing his rider with so much violence to the ground that he was unable to rise. All the French cavalry, in eager pursuit of the Prussians, passed by without recognising Blücher or even heeding him. His adjutant, who had contrived to remain near at hand, then procured him another horse, which he managed, though much bruised and shaken, to mount and rejoin his troops*—thus, probably, despoiling the French of the victory of the 18th.

For notwithstanding the secret plot that appears to have been organised to prevent Napoleon's orders from reaching his generals, or to confuse them by contradictory ones, yet for the second time on that fatal day he believed the

* Private letters of 1814 and 1815.

battle won. At three in the afternoon he despatched a courier to Paris to announce that victory was no longer doubtful. The emperor in
person was on the eve of completing it at the
head of the reserve forces when suddenly a brisk
fusilade was heard on the side towards St. Lam-
bert. "'Tis Grouchy," he exclaimed ; "the victory is ours!" A French writer * asserts that
Napoleon at that moment began whistling the
air, "*A la Monaco, l'on chasse et l'on déchasse,*"
interrupting it only to repeat, "*C'est Grouchy !
c'est Grouchy !*"

But, alas for him, it was not Grouchy! and a
few hours later, owing to this and other *contretemps*, resulting from indecision or treachery, not
only was the battle lost, but two-thirds of his
army were killed, wounded, or prisoners.

If ever the memoirs of M. de Talleyrand reveal
the truth, and nothing but the truth, concerning
his intriguing and eventful career, they may tell
who raised the fatal cry of "*Sauve qui peut !*" at
Waterloo, and throw a new light on the battle of
the 18th of June. But it is far more probable
that they will reveal nothing but a portrait of
himself, depicted after the manner in which he
would have posterity regard him and his many
doubtful acts.

As for Fouché, his treason was so evident to
all, that his and his accomplices' arraignment was

* Beaumont-Vassy, " *Mémoires secrets.*"

proposed by the Chamber of Deputies. Carnot publicly charged him with sacrificing both France and the emperor; Caulaincourt treated him with crushing disdain; and Général Grénier threatened to blow out his brains, but unfortunately did not carry out his threat.

Napoleon, the bearer of the news of his own defeat, arrived in Paris on the 21st. A panic seized the inhabitants when they heard of his return and that he had gone to the palace of the Élysée. Perhaps he preferred to dictate and sign there the act of abdication. " I offer myself," he said, " in sacrifice to the hatred of the enemies of France. My political life is ended, and I proclaim my son by the title of Napoleon II., Emperor of the French." While dictating this, the people had assembled round the Élysée, and were vociferously crying, " *Vive l'empereur !* "

Fouché therefore wrote to the English commander-in-chief to hasten the occupation of the capital, to prevent the French army, then reassembling in large numbers and perpetually crying, "*Vive l'empereur !* " from taking up arms, as they were ready to do for either Napoleon I. or Napoleon II.

All that concerns the Emperor Napoleon from his defeat at Waterloo to his departure for his miserable prison at Ste. Helena — that rock in a wide waste of waters — is too well known by all, it may be presumed, to need dwelling on here.

The hopeless exile to which he was doomed was indeed a melancholy close to the brilliant career of a man so eminently gifted; not merely as a military genius, but with qualities especially adapting him to be the ruler of a great nation.

CHAPTER XVI.

FOR the second time Paris is invested by foreign troops. They are swarming on the heights around it, and sharp conflicts are occurring between the invaders and the invaded. There is desperate skirmishing at St. Germain, and Versailles is taken and retaken again and again. Marshal Blücher's division sustains a partial defeat on the left bank of the Seine. He is attacked there by Général Exelmans with a detachment of six regiments of cavalry and one of infantry withdrawn from the command of the traitor Davoust. Supported, the French general could have annihilated the Prussian marshal's army.

But in vain, all in vain, is this sacrifice of brave men's lives in the desperate attempt to oppose the entry of the foreign hosts. In vain the Chambers

assemble, vote that Paris be put into a state of
siege, and call on the people and the army to rally
round "the tricoloured banner; consecrated by
the glory and the solemn oath of the nation." In
vain they proclaim the rights of Frenchmen, declare
their rejection of the Bourbons, their allegiance
to Napoleon II., and propose the appointment
of a council of regency; for an army of 150,000
men is at their gates. Napoleon II. is in his
enemies' safe-keeping. Talleyrand and Fouché
are plotting, caballing, striving — and for once in
their lives in concert — to overcome this strenuous resistance of the French people again to suc-
cumb to the yoke of the Bourbons.

In the wake of the Anglo-German army comes
Louis XVIII. — if not actually concealed in a
fourgon, yet screened from observation by the
baggage wagons that surround his closed carriage
and form his novel escort. But besides the
necessity for secretly bringing back this son of
Saint Louis to a people who declare that they will
not have him reign over them, there exists another
reason for sparing him as far as is possible all
excitement. He is suffering from bodily pain and
mental agitation, resulting from a paroxysm of
immoderate joy on learning that the allies were
victorious at Waterloo and the battle decisive. A
similar fit of frenzied delight had seized him in the
preceding year when informed that the throne of
France was vacant for him. But the present

attack has more lasting results; and from the period of the second restoration a degree of senility was sometimes painfully apparent in the excessive rage to which he would on mere fancied provocation give way, and his equally childish joy.

A rather amusing anecdote relating to his second return to Paris is told by the Comtesse de Bassanville. The king, in order to obtain some repose, and to prepare for the doubtful reception that might await him in Paris, stopped at the Château of Écouen, where, under the empire, the daughters of officers of the Legion of Honour were educated. During the attack on Paris they were sent to their homes for safety. The principal matron or governess also left, locking up her parrot in a large closet, with an ample supply of food for the short time she expected to be absent.

The chief bedchamber seems to have been that of the head matron, and on her couch Louis, tired with his journey, was soon reposing; his attendants temporarily leaving him to prepare the *en-cas*, or night meal, with which, like Louis XIV., the XVIIIth Louis of that royal line also regaled himself — once, twice, or thrice, as he chanced to awake, in the course of the night. Suddenly, and, as it seemed to him, close to his ear, in coaxingly whispered accents, he hears those hated words, " *Vive l'empereur!* " He is startled, of course; he listens, and would start upright on his couch, but unhappily he is unable to rise. " *Vive l'empe-*

reur!" again assails his ears, and this time with a
sort of chuckle at the end of it, a repetition of the
offensive words, and a hearty peal of laughter.

Who is this daring villain that thus presumes to
mock at and insult his sacred majesty?   "*Vive
l'empereur!*" is the screaming reply, "ha! ha!
ha!" The culprit seems to grow bolder each time
he repeats the offence, and indignation and rage
give strength to the king to find a bell-rope at the
head of the bed, at which he pulls most lustily.
The affrighted domestics hasten in.   No need to
inquire what has happened; Louis points towards
the spot whence come those sounds profane, so
joyously repeated.   They stand aghast; for the
laughter is louder, the tones more defiant.   The
king commands a search for the sacrilegious
offender.

He is neither under the bed nor behind it.   But
on drawing aside the curtains a door is seen; it is
locked, but soon yields to blows, when, swinging
in his cage, and excited by the noise, poor "Vert
Vert" is discovered gleefully laughing as he repeats the words which are the full extent of his
vocabulary and form the head and front of his
offending.   The conclusion is not pleasant.   The
offence of this imprudent imperialist was not con-
doned.   His neck was savagely twisted, and thus
he became the first victim of the second restoration.   Poor Vert Vert! Peace to his manes.

Louis remained at the Château of Écouen two

days, to recover from the shock his nerves had
sustained, also to see that all the ostentatiously
displayed crowned " N's," which, with derisive
pity, he pointed out to his indignant suite over
certain doors and entrances of this imperial insti-
tution, were thoroughly effaced.

But while the king was reposing, Paris continued in a very disturbed and unsettled state.
The commission of government recommended resistance, if need were, even unto death. Many of
the strong places of France also refused to surrender, and the general cry was, " The country
has been sold. *À bas les Bourbons ! Vive la nation !*" However, on the 3d of July, a capitulation — called a convention, to spare the feelings
of the Parisians — was agreed upon. The French
army to evacuate Paris in three days ; the main
body of the English and Prussian troops to occupy
it on the 6th ; and Louis — henceforth surnamed
"the Inevitable " — to enter on the 8th. He had,
however, stolen a march on rebellious Paris, and
was already at the Château d'Arnouville.

He was forming his new ministry there under
the inspiration of MM. de Talleyrand and Fouché,
who took their places — as of old under the
revolutionary government and the imperial *régime*
— of Minister of Foreign Affairs and Minister of
Police. A new favourite, M. Decazes, was named
Préfet of Police — M. de Talleyrand remarking of
him that he had the manners and appearance of a

barber's apprentice. As some far-seeing people perceived that M. Decazes was destined to become a personage of importance, Talleyrand's remark was treasured up by his enemies for use when needed; nor was it forgotten by Decazes himself, to whose ears it came.

The agents of the Duc d'Orléans had also taken advantage of the vehemence with which the return of Louis XVIII. was opposed, to put forward the claims of their patron, and had promised secretly to all parties the fulfilment of their wishes. Even the royalists were assured that if the crown were offered to the duke, he would accept it only to restore it to Louis XVIII. And there were many who, in their aversion to the latter, would have been willing that the Duc d'Orléans should supersede him. He of course did not openly appear in the matter. He watched and waited, and left the rest to his partisans, contenting himself with requesting the Duke of Wellington to take up his quarters at his Château of Neuilly. But the allies did not favour his pretensions; they were wholly intent on upholding the rights of legitimacy.

The proclamations concocted at Arnouville were therefore placarded on the walls of Paris as soon as the first instalment of 50,000 Prussian troops entered the city on the morning of the 6th to intimidate the people and to prevent their being torn down. But their acrimony was by no means abated by the tone of their gracious monarch's address to the French nation. It was commented upon in a very sarcastic spirit; and it was with many a jest, inspired by bitterness of feeling, that those gathered around these placards either read, or were informed by others, that " The king's powerful allies having dispersed the tyrant's satellites, he was hastening back to his dominions to reëstablish the constitution he had bestowed on France ; to repair the evil occasioned by the unaccountable revolt that had taken place, and by the war — its necessary result." It was further stated that he proposed " to recompense the faithful, and to put in force the existing laws against the guilty."

This reassuring document, dated from Câteau-Cambrésis, was signed in the usual imposing form — " Louis Stanislaus Xavier, by the grace of God King of France and Navarre," and " in the 20th year of our reign," of course — to be insisted on now more strenuously than ever. Some person or persons, however, soothed mortified feeling, it may be supposed, by tearing down part of the proclamations, and inserting in the greater number of those that remained the word " *l'Inévitable* " after the name, and " against the will of the nation " after " by the grace of God."*

But this futile demonstration of the people's discontent, though it may have relieved its agents of a little superfluous spleen, necessarily availed

* Private letters of 1814 and 1815.

not to change an iota of the programme of the two following days. On the 7th, another division of the Anglo-Prussian army, 50,000 strong, marched into Paris, and immediately began to conduct themselves most infamously, assuming the tone of masters in the houses where they were quartered. In the evening of the same day the enemy's artillery was heard rumbling and rolling over the stones with frightful *fracas*, as with boisterous triumph it was brought into Paris.

In 1814 the theatres were closed on the day of the entry of the hostile forces into the capital. On this occasion of still greater humiliation they were open, but by command, it was reported, in order to entice the people from the streets, where altercations were continually taking place between the populace and the insolent soldiery. It was certainly doing the Parisians but little injustice, considering with what rapture they had welcomed their conquerors in the preceding year, to suppose that any depression of feeling consequent on the country's misfortunes would vanish before the attractions of a play. It was to the interest of the royalist party, too, to encourage this feeling.

A French writer has recorded that when the cannon of the Anglo-German army was rolling with a noise like thunder along the streets of Paris, a crowded audience had assembled to witness at the theatre of the Porte Saint-Martin the *mélodrame* of the "*Pie voleuse*" (The Maid and the Magpie) ; and that so utterly devoid was this large audience of patriotic sentiments that the unwelcome sound raised in their stoical breasts no other feeling than a desire that the doors should be closed, as the noise prevented the actors from being distinctly heard.

The French people are certainly credited with great volatility of character and very elastic spirits. Yet if a private letter of the period may be credited — speaking generally, but referring it would seem to the occasion above mentioned — the narrator of the above must have been mis-informed. "It was a pleasant summer evening," says the writer ; "people of all classes were in the street, few being able to remain in their houses, listening in anxious suspense for what might occur or was occurring.

"A long train of artillery was coming in with a rolling, rushing, echoing sound like thunder, and shaking, as it seemed, the houses to their very foundations. Many made a precipitate re-treat ; others — women and children mostly — seemed for a moment panic-struck ; but perceiv-ing that the theatre opposite was open, they rushed in, followed by a few men, — fathers and husbands probably,— filled the staircases and pas-sages, and closed the doors."

If a large audience then filled the theatre, there, under these circumstances, they necessarily for a time were compelled to remain. This, too, appears to be the more natural occurrence; for at a time of such general agitation it seems incredible that a large number of people, brought together by chance, should one and all be so utterly insensible to their country's misfortune. It should, however, be remembered that there was a satisfied as well as a dissatisfied party; and that the Bourbons and their partisans, who had watched with fear and trembling the course of events, were glad to be brought back at any cost to the nation.

Louis XVIII. was again put in possession of the Tuileries on the 8th of July. He was accompanied by the Duke of Wellington and another 50,000 foreign troops; also by the announcement of a large pecuniary imposition, a military occupation, and the restitution of those treasures of art that formed the nation's most cherished trophies of its great captain's victories. It is not surprising, then, to find the people repudiating Louis XVIII., and leaving to foreigners the duty of escorting and welcoming him.

His newly appointed Préfet of the Seine was, of course, at the barrier of St. Denis to harangue his sovereign, and attended by such officials as could not absent themselves. The national guard abstained from assembling, because of an order from Général Dessoles to resume the white cockade. The city, from the Champs-Élysées to the extreme end of the Bois de Boulogne, presented the appearance of a vast camp. Troops were bivouacking on the quays, in the squares, and public gardens. Cannon was levelled on the Tuileries and at the points where two or more streets crossed each other, and English and Prussian soldiers were defiling on all sides, accompanied by drums and other military music.

The inhabitants were in constant terror from the pillaging propensities of this army of 170,000 troops of all nations, to whose tender mercies the capital seems to have been given up. Whatever they could lay their hands on in the houses where they were quartered, these conquering heroes carried off and sold. The Prussians indulged in the most savage reprisals. They attacked the public monuments, menaced the column of the grand army, and, had they not been prevented, would, at Marshal Blücher's suggestion, have blown up the bridges of Jena and Austerlitz. It is true that this ferocious old general was then suffering from one of those strange fits he was subject to, of confused thought bordering on mental alienation.

Notwithstanding these troubles, a few enthusiastic ladies of the extreme royalist party, who for the last twelve months had been vainly looking forward to the revival of the court of the old *régime*, imagined that this much-desired event could not now be far distant. "The usurper" was finally defeated, the king happily restored to his kingdom, and a royal marriage, if not exactly on the *tapis*, at all events prospectively so. They would, therefore, go forth to welcome the king, and show him that the ladies of the court, though neglected, were loyal. Arrayed in white silk, with lilies in their bonnets, and carrying each a bouquet of those rather flaunting white flowers, they await in the Tuileries gardens the king's return to his palace.

The fragrant spring violets with which those gardens so lately were covered have been carefully cleared away, and the bright summer sun now shines on the *fleur-de-lys*. Suddenly and secretly this change has been made, and appears to be a surprise to most people, whose pleasure or indignation is expressed as their sentiments are hostile or favourable to the king. Perhaps it was intended thus to console him for the disappearance of his cipher, his *fleur-de-lys*, and all emblems of the Restoration, which, during his absence, the people, with a sort of patriotic emulation, had effaced throughout Paris, just as he, hoping to obliterate the memory of Napoleon, had ordered the effacement of his cipher and emblems wherever they were met with. None, however, knew whence came the lilies, whose hand had planted them, or " whose was the treacherous thought " — as some who were present angrily exclaimed — " to pay this emblematic compliment to the king, regardless of the declared feeling of the nation."

This trifling incident might have resulted in an
émeute, or, at all events, in the lesser evil of the
total destruction of the flowers. But frowning
foreign troops were drawn up around the palace,
and a crowd had assembled, of whom but a few
probably felt very deeply concerning the offending
fleur-de-lys. They were far more anxious to see
" Louis l'Inévitable " — to support whose baseless
throne 100,000 men had just fallen victims —
reënter his palace as a conqueror. But it was
deemed advisable, as he could not walk in un-
assisted, that his entry should be effected rather
stealthily. As his foreign escort was so numerous,
his descent from his carriage was effectually concealed, and he was borne in easily and speedily.
His first appearance, then, was made in his chair,
wheeled into the balcony.

A shout, long and loud, of *" Vive le roi ! "*
greeted him, and — as appears to be always the
case on such occasions — " ' the air was rent ' with
the hearty acclamations of the people." A Prussian band struck up the eternal *" Vive Henri
Quatre ! "* with the inseparable *" Charmante
Gabrielle,"* which may have been meant as a compliment to Madame du Cayla, who, although not
visible, was quite within hearing of the joyous
strains which were sure to restore the people's
good humour.

The ladies in white who came to welcome back
the king, and who formed such a pretty group in

the midst of the lilies, apparently were not received into the palace. Bowing and curtseying, and waving small white scarfs, made up their greeting; which Louis graciously acknowledged by smiles and bows, a wave of the hand, and its momentary pressure on his heart. Nothing more, perhaps, could then well have been done. The king was tired; his couch was preparing. He had been rather frightened, too; but on the whole, if his welcome had not been warm, his return had been well got over, and he was prepared for a good night's rest.

The Ducs d'Angoulême and de Berry, unsuccessful in their attempt to propagate civil war in the southern, western, and northern departments, had repaired to the English headquarters at Louvres, returning to Paris with the army. The elder Bourbons are, therefore, in spite of the nation's resistance, once more installed in the capital. The intrigues of the Duc d'Orléans coming soon after to the king's ears, he is requested to return to England, and it is the king's declared intention that this wily candidate for his throne shall not be permitted to return to France.

Great rejoicings and numerous *fêtes* are in contemplation to cheer the spirits of his majesty's sorely tried faithful lieges, and generally to divert public attention from those signal punishments which are to "strike terror into the hearts of the guilty." The Emperor of Austria and the King

of Prussia, with the Emperor of all the Russias
(whose troops, though marching towards Belgium,
did not arrive in time to take part in the Waterloo
battle), are daily expected in Paris to celebrate the
abasement of France.   The beginning of a new
reign of terror is also at hand.   "We are going to
punish, and punish severely," is the announcement
of the pious Duchesse d'Angoulême — her countenance more radiant than her friends have before
seen it since her return to France.   Her words
are widely circulated — exultingly by the Bourbonites ; by others, to friends as a warning ; and
they obtain for the revengeful daughter of Marie
Antoinette the unenviable sobriquet of "Catherine
de' Médici the Second."

CHAPTER XVII.

O sooner were the allied armies again in possession, than the English, who had fled with such haste on the approach of Napoleon, were crowding back to the French capital. Great gaieties were expected to follow the second restoration, the general peace, and the return of the emperors, kings, and princes to Paris. The *modistes* and *couturières*, with similar expectations, were inventing new fashions to harmonise with this looked-for revival of the too long suspended amenities of social life.

The white banner, flaunting again on the Vendôme column, brought white dresses into favour ; and the season allowed of their general adoption, as well as of white bonnets, white veils, white fans, gloves, and parasols. Virgin white was encountered at every turn; and such was the general passion for white that the sanguinary deeds then committing in the South were distinguished by the name of the " White Terror."

Unchecked by the government, a sort of " St. Bartholomew" ensued, and crimes the most atrocious were perpetrated with impunity during this royalist reaction.   None, without shuddering with horror, can read of the ferocious cruelties inflicted on Protestants and Bonapartists, as their victims were classed, by these partisans of the monarchy by right divine.   The vile deeds of the Terror of 1793 under the Jacobin Robespierre were not more revolting to humanity, nor is any crime recorded of it more savage, more ferociously barbarous, then the horrible assassination of Maréchal Brune by the White Terrorists at Avignon.   The blood runs cold at the mere thought of their murders by fire and sword, their exultation over the agony of their victims, and their demoniacal dances and songs.

As far as possible these excesses were concealed from the general public by false accounts in the government papers.   But if there were attempts at gaiety in Paris they were confined to the foreign visitors and invaders; for, except the extreme royalists, few beside participated in them.

The Duke of Wellington soon after his entry gave a grand ball; but invitations to it were rarely accepted by the French.   Those who did attend "compared themselves to victims asked to dance on the tomb of their country." There was a superabundant display of lilies, real and artificial, on this occasion, but chiefly on the dresses of the English ladies, who, with their accustomed good taste, were wreathed and garlanded, festooned and draped, with these floral emblems to the fullest possible extent. A simple bouquet, or single "sacred flower" worn in the hair, sufficed, in most instances, to attest the loyalty of the *élégantes* of the French *beau monde*.

Two or three there were, indeed, whose luke-warm royalism led them to substitute the modest lily-of-the-valley for the consecrated emblem of purity that descended from heaven on the sainted monarch who first bore it on his banner. But this ingenious attempt to defraud royalty of its due, be assured, would not pass unnoticed. The austere countenance of the resentful duchess would plainly indicate to those ladies, when next they presumed to pay their respects at the Tuileries, that their disloyal act was not unknown to her. Keen, far-seeing eyes, and acute ears, were present at all social gatherings to detect and report on the words and deeds and looks — one might almost say, and to read the thoughts, which were certainly often guessed at — of the company present. Unfortunately, however, this sort of espionage has been common to every *régime* in France.

Many of the English aristocracy were then in Paris, and received each other; "as, in the *haute société française*, the women made it a rule that no one should propose the introduction of a foreign lady." To be reminded of their emigration, it was said, was not agreeable to them. And as to their debts of friendship, if they did not altogether repudiate, they barely acknowledged them, and avoided any renewal of intimacy with their former friends. It is surprising to find French royalists returning to their country cherishing the same prejudices against the English and holding the same illiberal opinions concerning them as had been current in France before the revolution.

With Bonapartists, republicans, and some other sections of the political world, hatred of the English would be explicable. Not so with royalist emigrants, who probably would never have seen their country again had England made peace with Napoleon (the better course for France, at all events, as some persons have thought), instead of assisting to restore the expelled dynasty. But whether or not, all parties were agreed in cordially detesting their conquerors, English and German, from the commanders-in-chief, their officers and troops, even to the most humble private traveller. As regards the military, there appears to have been very sufficient reason for general dissatisfaction; their extortion of sums of money and their wholesale plundering were shameful;

and they received no check from their commanders.

It seems strange that the Duke of Wellington
should have expected — as it appears he did expect — to find the favour he coveted in the eyes
of Madame Récamier by "exclaiming with much
elation," as, after his return from Waterloo, he
entered her *salon*, "I have beaten him ; thoroughly
beaten him!" Madame Récamier has herself
recorded that she was "deeply pained." On the
former triumphant occasion, when introduced to
her, she had not received him with that habitual
sympathetic warmth of manner which with the
charm of her beauty brought so many slaves to
her feet. He was piqued at this coldness. But
now he imagines all reserve will vanish. For he
comes crowned with fresh laurels, announcing
himself a victor, and claiming as his reward the
approving smiles of beauty, as, bowing the knee
before her, he seeks permission to kiss her hand.
But she concedes neither. Before all things she
is a Frenchwoman ; and he learns, apparently with
surprise as well as mortification, that she is too
profoundly grieved at the degradation of her
country to feel flattered by the victor's homage.

But Madame Récamier, who so entirely monop-
olised the attention of the gentlemen, young and
old, *grands seigneurs* and men of humbler position,
learned and unlearned, wealthy and poor, and of
every nation, was often severely criticised by the

ladies, who accused her of being, under those soft winning ways of hers, the most artful as well as heartless of coquettes. Miss Berry, who was then in Paris, speaking of a reception at Madame Récamier's, says: "She was reclining on a *chaise longue*, with twelve or fifteen men in adoration around her. Only three or four ladies present." Miss Berry, however, did not greatly admire her. Yet she had seen her in 1802, after the peace of Amiens, when she was in the full bloom of her beauty, being then but twenty-five.

"I met her," she says, "at a dinner at Mr. Francis Jackson's. She has the finest house in Paris, in the new style, and is herself *the* decided beauty of the *new* world ; for if she can be called handsome, she is entirely a *figure de fantaisie*. Her complexion is clear, she is young and tall, and dressed, with much affectation of singularity, in the extravagance of fashion. Her manners are *doucereuses*, thinking much of herself, with perfect carelessness about others. She has pretensions, I understand, to *bel esprit*, besides being a beauty ; and they may be as well founded, yet not sufficient to burn her for a witch." This, perhaps, is not quite a faithful portrait ; but women rarely do admire those of their own sex who usurp the admiration of men so unconscionably as did Madame Récamier.

Instances of a woman exciting such general admiration and devoted passionate love are, however,

very rare. Yet her reputation remained unblem-
ished; the tongue of scandal breathed no word
against her fair fame, and that at a time when im-
morality was the rule of life. That she was to
blame in giving tacit encouragement to the ardent
passion of Benjamin Constant, she herself, some
few years later, acknowledged. But at the period
now in question — 1815 — he was still in the
agony of unrequited love, and still in Paris, hoping
that a chance yet remained to him of being called
upon to lay his head on the fatal block, or to bare
his breast to receive death from the bullets of a
party of soldiers.

Only thus, he believed, could he inspire that
cold bosom with pity — love he no longer looked
for — and draw the tribute of a tear to his melancholy fate from the bright eyes that were not
often reddened by tears. He has informed Madame Récamier of the Duchesse d'Angoulême's
widely circulated announcement, "*Nous allons
punir, et punir beaucoup.*" But Madame Récamier
was not willing to have his death on her conscience. She implores him to leave Paris. "Madame Constant de Rebecque is anxiously awaiting
him in Brussels. Let him depart and ease her
fears, while yet there is time." Not he. He will
await the publication of the general amnesty, trust-
ing to find himself on the list of those excluded
from benefiting by it. For Benjamin Constant, in
his adherence to Napoleon, has been more consist-

ent than many others who declared in his favour
on his return from Elba.   He has publicly stated
that the compact accepted and sworn to by the
emperor and the people, in the Champ de Mars
on the 1st of June, could not be annulled by the
defeat of Waterloo.

This sentiment, however honourable to him, of
itself, would suffice to render him odious in the
eyes of the king, who had obtained a law, voted
unanimously and with much exultation by an obsequious royalist Chamber, declaring that "death
was the only penalty that could atone for the un-
speakable crime of aiding and abetting the guilty
designs of the usurper."   Thus Louis was able to
exclude from his "*general* amnesty" fifty-seven
leading men, whose ability or influence might be
prejudicial to his and his family's designs.   But as
these assassinations must be perpetrated in Paris,
their infamy was to be in some degree masked by
conducting them under a judicial form.

What a spectacle to offer the gay throng who,
on pleasure bent, then filled every room, from
ground floor to the eighth or ninth story, of every
house in Paris that had not been fully taken possession of by the soldiers of the foreign armies!
Then there was the spoliation of the museums
and national libraries.   At this Paris stood aghast!
Rage filled every Frenchman's breast, so deeply
was the national pride wounded, and curses loud
and deep were poured on the heads of the allies.

All other miseries, even the millions of the indemnity and the presence and maintenance of the army of occupation, seemed to sink into insignificance compared with this one great humiliation.

For besides being trophies of the victories of the French arms, the greater part ceded to France by the Treaty of Tolentino, those fine productions of Raphael, Pietro de Cortoni, Correggio, Canachi, and other eminent masters of the old Italian school, when removed from Italy were fast going to destruction from extreme neglect. It was necessary, either carefully to restore, to clean, or in some cases, as the only means of saving them, to transfer these *chefs-d'œuvre* to new canvas before they could be publicly exhibited. It was then for the first time that their beauty became apparent to their former possessors, who now clamoured for their return, together with the ancient sculpture, whose dilapidations had been treated with similar care, occupying, with the pictures, many able artists a period of two years to complete. Even Louis XVIII., so anxious to get rid of everything recalling the memory of the "usurper," as he invariably termed his great predecessor, was very loth to part with these memorials of the usurper's victories.

Their removal was effected under the superintendence of Canova, the emperor's liberally patronised and favourite sculptor. "No Frenchman," says an eye-witness* of these scenes of lamentation and despair on the one part and of ruffianly insolence on the other, "would aid in this work. Promises of reward, threats of punishment, were alike ineffectual. Porters, labourers, men plying for work, would not, indeed, dared not — such was the exasperation of the people — render any assistance to the spoilers. The Murillos had chiefly fallen to the share of the generals; but, though considered private property, their restitution was demanded and obtained."

It was found necessary to surround the Place du Carrousel and the entrances to the Louvre with troops, to keep off the French; only foreigners were allowed to pass in while the Venus and Apollo were being put into their cases, or coffins. Artists wept over them and passionately kissed them, as though separating from loved friends. Austrian cavalry were stationed around while Austrian workmen brought down the famous "Horses of the Sun" from the arch of the Carrousel. It had been attempted in the night, lest royal eyes should be offended, royal feelings wounded. But the attempt was unsuccessful. It appears to have been attended with great difficulty, increased by the repeated attempts of the people to enter the place in spite of the cavalry.

At last the descent of the steeds was accomplished. But before they were unharnessed,

* Helen Maria Williams, Letters, etc.

English ladies, who were present to witness as a morning's amusement a scene so painful to French ladies, are said to have "placed themselves triumphantly in the Car of Victory, to which Napoleon had attached the famous bronze horses." * Of course the ambition of these English ladies did not add either to their own or their nation's popularity at that critical period, Many similar scenes occurred in Paris at this time, very distressing to some persons, very gratifying to the bad feeling of others.

The 2,000 MSS. from the Vatican, which were part of the spoils of the Thirty Years' War, presented to the Pope by General Tilly, but ceded to France by the Treaty of Tolentino, were claimed by the Margrave of Baden, whose claim, it appears, was allowed. There were even claimants for the cabinet of natural history in the Jardin des Plantes. To cover the bare walls of the museum, the spoilers were good enough to leave the ancient tapestry, said to have been worked by the queen of William the Norman and her ladies, representing the taking of the city of London and other of his conquests in England.

The Parisians had hoped much from the interference of the Emperor Alexander, who in the previous year had played the part of King of Paris with such general approbation, and was confessedly so French in his sympàthies. Count

* Helen Maria Williams, Letters, etc.

Nesselrode, in the emperor's name, did represent
to Lord Castlereagh that the whole proceeding
was inexpedient, but simply because it would
place Louis XVIII. in an unpleasant position as
regarded the public. But Lord Castlereagh had
already urged in favour of the restitution of the
Italian pictures, etc., that "it would be more
advantageous for the arts to be cultivated in
Rome." There the matter ended.

But Alexander had really less influence on the
present than on the former occasion. His troops
were withdrawn, not having been engaged at
Waterloo. It was, besides, apparent to the ladies
who had been most eager to welcome him back —
fancying that on his reappearance the *fêtes* and
rejoicings would begin in good earnest — that a
very marked change had come over him. There
was no abatement in the general courtesy of his
manners, but there was certainly a falling off in
that gallantry which was so flattering even to
those who were not the most marked objects of
his attention. Some thought that he was annoyed
that his troops had missed their share of the
honours of Waterloo ; others that he had adopted
a serious air as being more suited to the title of
"*Blessed*," which, with a sort of political canoni-
sation, had been decreed him by the Senate of St.
Petersburg.

The emperor had, however, declined to accept
that strange title, — it being inconsistent, he said,

with the simplicity and moderation of which he had desired to set the nation an example. But disappointed society was not destined long to remain in doubt as to the cause of the change so deeply lamented in their former "adorable emperor."

Following quickly on his arrival was the reappearance of Madame de Krüdener in Paris ; and if the *salons,* where so many bright eyes once welcomed him, had lost their charm for the melancholy czar, the society of that mystical lady had become especially attractive to him. At Heilbronn she at last succeeded in throwing her spell over him. "A message from heaven," says M. Eynard, her fullest biographer and firmest believer in what she termed her mission, "sent her thither, having numberless and wonderful things to tell him." It was, however, only by stratagem that she obtained her first interview with him, when, "tearing the veil from his eyes, she showed him that he was a sinner." A long sermon followed ; and, according to M. Eynard, "he listened attentively to it, concealed his face with his hands, and wept abundantly."

"Madame," he said, after their interview had lasted three hours, "Madame, your words are music to my soul. I beg that our interviews may be frequently renewed, and that you will not leave Heilbronn." At Heidelberg, whither she followed, the same sort of intercourse took place, he entreat-

ing the support of her presence, she vaunting him
as "great, great with the greatness of a Christian."
Apart from her mysticism and the spiritual communication she professed to hold with heaven, she
did some good at Heidelberg and elsewhere — visiting the prisons and reading the Scriptures to
criminals under sentence of death.

In Paris Madame de Krüdener found more difficulty in keeping her imperial convert within the
charmed circle of her influence. "It required,"
says M. Eynard, "a tact that only the Spirit of
God could inspire ; for she was in danger of losing
him either by too much severity or by permitting
too much laxity." She took advantage of those
fits of melancholy that occasionally came over him
when recalling with remorse his complicity in his
father's downfall. Then she subjugated him entirely. At other times she flattered his immense
amour propre by assuring him that he was the
angel destined to carry out the will of the Lord on
earth.

Their mysterious intercourse gave rise to much
curiosity in Paris. And when it was discovered
that they passed the evening in reading the Bible,
Madame interpreting it according to instructions
received direct in poetical visions from heaven,
"visions or hallucinations resembling in their extravagance those of Swedenborg, but minus their
obscenity and revolting horrors," a sort of indignant pity was felt for the czar's blindness and

folly. Jokes at his expense, both mirthful and sarcastic, were, however, not spared. Nor did the *beau monde* spare the lady, the depravity of whose early life had caused much scandal, even in dissipated Paris and other capitals, in the period preceding the empire. The story of the strange steps she had taken in 1803 to secure success for her novel of " *Valérie* " was revived, and obtained a revival of its popularity. It is said to be the account of her own career, much poetised of course, and told in the form of letters. She was desirous of literary fame at that time, and, as she was wealthy, she employed poets to write enthusiastic sonnets addressed to her in the public prints. In Paris she inquired at the most fashionable shops for *toilettes à la Valérie* — bonnets, *fichus*, gloves, etc. — and as they had not been heard of, she described and ordered them. Forthwith they appeared, and with the *toilette* the novel also became known and in vogue.

But although society laughed at the now rigid priestess and her imperial convert, and amused themselves greatly over the exaggerated reports of their proceedings, yet curiosity drew many to the religious meetings or receptions of this repentant Magdalen. She had a fine hôtel in the Faubourg St. Honoré, its gardens then extending to the Champs-Élysées. There she and the emperor walked in the evening, discoursing probably on the prescribed form of the Holy Alliance which was shortly to be the result of her influence, or on the New Jerusalem, which the initiated understood to be the symbol of a social renovation or revolution she aspired either to establish or lead.

All were welcomed who chose to attend her receptions, her object being to gain proselytes. The entertainment consisted of alternate prayer and preaching, during which her professed followers knelt. Having a great flow of passionate eloquence, and a vivid imagination, she sometimes acquired a fleeting influence over those of her auditors who were sentimentally inclined. Yet generally she made more impression on men than on her own sex. Some accounts speak of her as a woman of imposing appearance ; but the descriptions of her person by two individuals who knew her well and conversed with her often are so entirely different that it is impossible to reconcile them as describing the same person.

Mademoiselle de Cochelet, one of the ladies of Queen Hortense, speaking of her when at Carlsruhe — she was anxious to find a convert in the ex-queen — says : " Her small, slight figure and extreme spareness (*sa petite taille mince, son excessive maigreur*, etc.), her fair hair, in the greatest disorder, and the animated expression of her eyes, imparted to her person a sort of supernatural air." Her fanatical disciple, M. Eynard, says she was "tall (*de grande taille*), of dusky complexion, with protruding lips, large blue eyes, charming fair hair, and arms of real beauty." He adds: "She was a very rich heiress;" and it appears that in Geneva and other places, whence the police expelled her, she bought most of her proselytes.

Her mode of impressing those who attended her *séances* in Paris was to stand in a sort of dim religious light, obtained by the artificial arrangement of lamps and draperies, at the end of a succession of *salons* widely opening into each other. There, kneeling, with upraised eyes and arms, she prayed with much apparent fervour. Afterwards, advancing to the next *salon*, she began to preach, growing more excited as she proceeded, and generally concluding with a denunciation of the wickedness of the age and a prediction of the approaching end of the world.

Benjamin Constant was much impressed by her ecstatic performances. She charged him with what he termed a most embarrassing commission — a request to Madame Récamier that if she visited her again to come less beautiful, as she distracted people's attention. "You cannot, of course, divest yourself of your charms," he wrote to Madame Récamier, "but do try not to heighten them."

CHAPTER XVIII.

THOUGH the streets of Paris had perhaps never before been so thronged, yet the throng for the most part was a very unwelcome one. Though there was no lack of bustle and activity in the city, yet it was not due to increased briskness of trade, but to the hurrying to and fro, and in all directions, of agents and porters employed by "the allied enemies," as the favourite phrase was, bearing away the art treasures torn from the Paris museums. An unaccustomed gloom hung over the capital. Pleasure was said to have emigrated, while many called pleasure the fifty-eighth victim of the general amnesty.

The spirits of the Parisians were saddened by

what was passing around them, by the news that every post brought of the terrible reprisals in La Vendée and elsewhere; and they mourned by anticipation over the victims whose blood was to be shed in their midst — to be poured forth as a libation to appease the wrath of the son of Saint Louis. But let them repress their murmurs, and give no expression to their feelings, for the duch-ess's order has gone forth to "resent all insulting cries."

Perhaps comfort may be derived from the thought that some of the victims will escape; for Fouché, the powerful Minister of Police, even he has shrunk from putting into execution the Draconian law of the royalist chambers. Before signing the order for the arrest of the fifty-seven victims — mark how scrupulously conscientious he had become — *before* signing the king's order for their arrest, it is asserted that he signed fifty-seven passports, and warned those to whom they were despatched to put themselves out of danger; and, lest funds for the purpose should not at the moment be readily obtainable, he enclosed a sum sufficient to enable them to reach the frontier — as much, it is said, as 500,000 *francs* (20,000*l.* sterling).

It is to be hoped this is true, and that, having done so much harm, he sought by doing a little good to make some slight atonement. He had just married his second wife, Mdlle. de Castellane.

The lady was neither youthful nor rich, but of a very noble royalist family. Yet she disdained not the title of Duchesse d'Otranto, to which a disgraceful notoriety, rather than honour, was attached. The marriage of this red-handed revolutionist was quite a grand affair, with all the old *régime* ceremonial. The Comte d'Artois was present, and signed the marriage contract. Some accounts assert that the king's signature was also attached to it. This is doubtful, however, for Louis detested Fouché; but it is certain that the greater part of the Faubourg St. Germain assisted at the ceremony. Fouché thought to sustain himself by this alliance at the court of the Restoration. Nevertheless, his days as Minister of Police were numbered.

But Fouché's generosity and desire to save life on the occasion of his marriage availed but little. Few of the doomed victims cared to escape, and fewer still to accept a pecuniary gift from Fouché to enable them to profit by his warning. Général de La Bédoyère, who disdained to hide himself in the provinces, was the first to suffer; and it was he whom the restored monarch was anxious first to strike. He and his troops marched out of Grenoble to meet the emperor, and joined him before he entered the town. He was also urgent in his efforts to obtain the recognition of Napoleon II. by the provisional government, and committed the further offence of remaining faithful to the emperor in his adversity and accompanying him to Rochefort.

He was not allowed to offer any explanation of his conduct, and of course he was condemned to death. Many friends strove to save him. Even Madame de Krüdener interposed, and appealed to the Duchesse d'Angoulême. She might as well have appealed to one of the stone statues in the Tuileries gardens. Alexander also, in the presence of the princess, blamed both the arrest and the sentence of La Bédoyère, and pleaded for clemency.

"Why employ so much severity?" he said; "and what good can it lead to?"

"Sire," replied the duchess, "justice requires firmness and measures calculated to inspire awe."

"Madame, if justice has its rights, clemency also claims hers," said the emperor.

"Clemency," she answered, "is the equivalent of weakness."

"You mistake, madame; clemency, or charity, will gain hearts, and will subdue them," rejoined the emperor. But such sentiments had no place in the breast of the duchess. She breathed only vengeance.

La Bédoyère met his fate with much calmness and courage. But when, having disposed of him, the Chambers again met, there appeared to be a chance of M. Benjamin Constant becoming the interesting individual he was anxious to be, in order to inspire that tender pity which claims close kindred with love. Violent royalists declared that he deserved the same fate as La Bédoyère. However, as his name was not on the fatal list, he was not molested, — purposely overlooked, perhaps,— his facile pen being wanted. He had already written a panegyric on the king, and allowed Madame Récamier to see it. "If it were known," he said, "that I had written it, I should at once be accused of wanting to sell myself. But it is to you only that I make this offer, and you refuse to buy me."

The next victim was Maréchal Ney, "bravest of the brave." Arrested in the department of Cantal, he was transferred to Paris, to be interrogated first by the king's favourite, "the simpering Decazes," then by a council of war — probably by way of further humiliating the marshal, and adding a sharper sting to his mental torture; for his sentence was already pronounced, his condemnation being made a question of state by the king, the Comte d'Artois, and the Duchesse d'Angoulême. She, unhappy woman, was wondrously active in baffling the efforts of friends and relatives to save the lives of the condemned men, or to spare them any added ignominy to the sentence of death. Marie Antoinette was never more persistent in obtaining grants of money and pensions to heap on her worthless favourites, regardless of the poverty of the state and the sufferings of the people, than was her daughter at this period in slaying — so far as countenancing such deeds availed — all who had been guilty of serving their old master with more fidelity than the new one.

There was some difficulty in assembling a council of war to try the great marshal. Many officers begged to be excused from being included in it; others declined, for they were bound to condemn, while they desired to acquit him, but had not the courage to do so. The oldest of the marshals, Maréchal Moncey, was chosen president, when at last seven officers were prevailed on to form a council. But the veteran soldier absolutely refused, and informed the king of his resolve. At the same time he pleaded nobly and courageously for the accused marshal.

"Reflect, Sire," he wrote, "reflect on this matter. Believe me, it is both dangerous and impolitic to drive brave men to desperation. Ah! it might well have been that the unfortunate Maréchel Ney, if he had shown at Waterloo that decision he so many times before displayed elsewhere, instead of being dragged before a military commission, would have been implored by those who now seek his death to extend protection to them." The magnanimous Louis was astounded at the old marshal's presumption. The reply to his letter was an announcement of his degradation in military rank and condemnation to three months' imprisonment.

The seven officers who formed the military commission, having gone through the form of interrogating Ney, declared, by a vote of five against two, that they were not competent to be his judges, — thus transferring the odium of condemning him to the Chamber of Peers, — Ney being a peer of France. The Duc de Richelieu appeared as his accuser.

"We come," he said, addressing the assembled peers, "not in the name of the king only, but also in the name of France, indignant and amazed at the crime, and even in the name of Europe, to adjure and require you to judge the Maréchal Ney." The marshal's advocates, MM. Berryer and Dupin, saw at once that there was no hope for the accused; for to judge meant in this case to condemn. But Dupin pleaded that Sarrelouis, Ney's birthplace, by the late convention was no longer a part of France. Ney, replying to this plea, said, "I am a Frenchman. I shall die free. My appeal is to Europe and posterity."

Most of the peers of the empire declined to vote; the ecclesiastical peers took no part in the proceedings. Seventeen others voted for banishment; but for death the majority, in compliance with the royal wish, was overwhelming. It was, however, hoped — against hope, probably — that the sentence alone would satisfy the king. Immediately, therefore, the most strenuous efforts were made to obtain its remission. But when those who came to plead for the life of a great and brave man arrived at the palace, his gracious majesty was going to bed (the execution was to take place at dawn on the following morning), and would not even listen to a word they had to say. Waving his hand as he was wheeled away, he exclaimed, "Let me hear when I awake that the traitor has paid the forfeit of his crime!"

The people of "indignant France" uttered the word "rescue!" Secretly the scene of the murder was then changed from the plain of Grenelle to the esplanade facing the Observatory, and the deed fixed to take place half an hour earlier. The marshal seemed surprised on alighting from his carriage, but observed, with a peculiar smile, as guessing the reason, "It is to be done here, is it?" Then placing himself against the wall opposite the twelve reluctant assassins, "Soldiers!" he said, "do your duty — straight to the heart!" Twelve balls pierced him, and, as he fell, he exclaimed, "*Vive la France!*" He was buried next day, without any ceremony, at Père-Lachaise, while the police were busy in effacing the blood of the "bravest of the brave" from the wall against which, in his 46th year, he was shot.

A few weeks earlier, after many romantic adventures, there perished at Pizzo, at the same age and in the same manner, by order of Ferdinand, the restored King of Naples, a former brother-in-arms of Maréchal Ney — Joachim Murat, the

" Achilles," as he was called, of the French army. He was shot in less than half an hour after sentence of death was pronounced. He met his fate very courageously ; and, with something of the romance with which all his acts were tinged, he died holding in his hand a cornelian cameo head of his wife. Thinking, too, a little of his personal appearance after death (he was a handsome man), he exclaimed, as he bared his breast to receive the bullets, " Soldiers ! spare the face — aim at the heart."

Many executions which throughout the country had caused more or less sensation had taken place. Yet there remained two or three individuals of note still at large, when the question of the expediency of finding a wife for the Duc de Berry was again seriously discussed. The Grand Duchess Anne, the Emperor Alexander's youngest sister, was first thought of. She was on the cards when Napoleon was looking around the courts of Europe for a youthful bride, and had now just attained her twenty-first year. She was extremely handsome ; but she was not a Roman Catholic, and the empress dowager, her mother, was unwilling that she should become one. Of greater importance still, M. de Talleyrand had so flattered Louis XVIII.'s absurd pride in his ancient and saintly descent, when formerly discussing this marriage question, that a doubt now suggested itself to the royal mind of the eligibility of a member of so *parvenu* a family as the Romanoffs for the honour of being the bride of a Bourbon.

It was, however, most desirable — the throne being now so firmly rooted in the affections of the people — that the elder branch of the royal line should not die out. Of the occurrence of this melancholy event there seemed to be every chance; for no youthful heir was expected from the Angoulêmes; and the dissipated De Berry appeared satisfied with his left-handed union, and much attached to his English wife and his children. The Comte d'Artois was therefore urged again to enter the holy estate of matrimony, and to seek a bride among the youthful princesses of Europe. But he, alas! was already bound by solemn vows to his heavenly bride, the Comtesse de Polastron.

Besides the one cogent reason for enlarging the family circle, there was another of considerable weight. Louis began to perceive that the court of the Tuileries was a court only in name, and that even the exclusives of the Faubourg St. Germain were suspected of looking back with regret to the brilliant court of the empire. In this dilemma, he consulted Madame du Cayla; who told him that the only way of bringing back mirth and gaiety to the now silent salons of the royal dwelling, and probably securing also the much-desired heir — to the discomfiture of his serene highness of Orléans — was to find forth-

with a young and sprightly Duchesse de Berry.
Her counsels, always prudent, always convincing
to the king, are agreed to.   But before the marriage bells can be rung, certain matters of state
must be settled.   M. Blacas-d'Aulps, with whom
the ministry will not transact business, all favourite and old friend though he is, is dismissed at
the fair countess's suggestion.   He is sent to
Rome — which in his case is equivalent to being
sent to Coventry, but with an ample fortune to
console him — to urge the Pope on the subject of
the Concordat, and — vainly, as it proves — on
that of the 19th year and the coronation.

The two men who have made themselves Louis's
stepping-stones to the throne are also to be discarded.   In vain they have turned their coats
and sought to justify their position in the new
order of things — Talleyrand, by informing the
king how France should now be governed, and by
endeavouring to obtain more favourable terms
from the allies for their aid in getting rid of the
"usurper"; and Fouché, who as he drew nearer
to the close of his career would seem to have
become sick of blood and outrage, by laying
before the king a truly pathetic picture of the
state to which unhappy France and her people
were reduced.

Fouché, who, by means of his well-trained
agents and perfectly organised system of police,
knew everything that was said or done, or pro-

posed to be done, in Paris, and indeed throughout France, was well aware that there was a cabal against him, and that his dismissal was imminent. He therefore at once placed the king in a dilemma by a premature request to accept his resignation and to appoint him his representative at the Saxon court.   There were individuals in the government who thought the affairs of France must come to a standstill if Fouché did not hold office.   Hence the king's perplexity.   He, however, took the opportunity of appointing his favourite Decazes to fill the vacant post of Minister of Police.   There was also a plot on foot to assassinate Fouché on his journey, but he amused himself by effectually thwarting it.   When, some months later, the law disqualifying "conventionalists and regicides" from holding any office under the government deprived him of his post at the Saxon court, Fouché retired, first to Prague, then to Lintz, to live *en prince* on his immense private fortune.*

M. de Talleyrand pursued a contrary plan. He clung to his *portefeuille* of foreign affairs, and had the mortification of being told by the king that a change in the ministry would alone obtain some favourable terms from the allies.   Stung to the quick in his *amour propre* as a diplomatist, he

---

* He died in 1820, aged 66, at Trieste, of a pulmonary complaint. Though so infamous in his public career, he is said to have been most estimable in his domestic relations.

then offered his resignation. In his most gracious manner, and with many acknowledgments for thus sacrificing himself to reasons of state, Louis smilingly took M. de Talleyrand at his word, and transferred his *portefeuille* to the hands of the Duc de Richelieu.

The great influencè which the Comtesse du Cayla had obtained over the mind of Louis XVIII. was very evident in this political intrigue. In secret intelligence with the Emperor Alexander and the Duc de Richelieu, she had prepared the fall of the ministry, and induced him to favour a new one of purely royalist principles ; and she is said to have owed this singular empire over him far less to her beauty than to her tact. What he had refused the Comte d'Artois and the Duchesse d'Angoulême, he at her persuasion consented to. She passed two hours with him daily in literary conversation, criticising the works of the day, and repeating stanzas of the poetry of other days.

Political subjects were supposed to be forbidden. Yet she contrived to introduce lively remarks on the events of the time, and generally succeeded, by a sort of refined cajolery in which she was an adept, in bringing him over to her views. It was his habit to affect to defer to them from gallantry, but usually he yielded to her wishes, whatever they chanced to be. She obtained from him the pardon of the Duc de Rovigo — Général Savary — who, as Minister of Police,

Talleyrand.
Photo-etching after the painting by Lacour.

had never refused her a passport for Holland when her health needed change of air. As he was attached to Napoleon, and she was very assiduous in her attendance at the imperial court, he may not have suspected that from Holland she passed over to England.

At all events, she was sufficiently grateful for her passport to save the general's life. On the other hand, she is accused of having had a part in preparing the list of the fifty-seven who were excepted from the general amnesty. But this may not be true; for, as a court favourite, and the *amie du cœur* of an old dotard, she naturally had many enemies.

The men chosen to form the new cabinet had all given proofs of pure royalism during the Hundred Days. It included a traitor duke of the empire, Général Clarke, Duc de Feltre. Yet so extremely pure were they that exception was taken to M. Decazes, formerly Madame Lætitia's secretary, afterwards Louis Bonaparte's representative in Paris when King of Holland. He had worn the tricoloured cockade as captain of the 2d legion of the national guard, but exchanged it for a white one when he found that white was the winning colour.

On Napoleon's arrival from Elba, Decazes was present when the magistrates of the Supreme Court assembled to vote an address to him. When he expressed some disapproval of the lan-

guage employed, it was replied that "he who
had been able to reconquer his kingdom without
difficulty, and in the course of a rapid march,
might well be termed its legitimate sovereign."
"I never before heard," he answered, audaciously,
"that legitimacy was the prize of a race."

The government of the Hundred Days thought
it worth while to invite him to take up his abode
at a distance of forty leagues from the capital.
This brought him into favour with Louis XVIII.,
and obtained for him the post of Préfet of Police.
In this capacity he still further won the royal
favour by placing before the king in piquant language a sort of daily *chronique scandaleuse* of the
capital.   His winning manners completed the conquest.   He seems to have imitated Madame Récamier, and has been compared to her, in the warm
interest he affectedly evinced towards all he came
in contact with, seizing both hands of utter strangers in his eager sympathy, and looking into their
eyes with a kind of earnest pleasure as he listened
to the most commonplace utterances.

The fair countess regarded M. Decazes with no
friendly eye.   His growing favour alarmed her,
and secretly she strove to undermine his credit
with the king.   In this manner she obtained toleration for herself with the count and the duchess
and the Pavillon Marsan circle generally, who dis-
liked both these favourites, and hoped to secure
the *congé* of both by the cordial dislike they enter-

tained for each other. But nothing of the sort occurred. The countess, as the king's *spirituelle amie intime*, remained *maîtresse-en-titre* to the end; while M. Decazes, confirmed in his post of Minister of Police, with the direction — as the king added, laying some stress on the words — of the " *travail secret* " of his department, continued some years in office.

When a change came, he was far too important and wealthy a personage to fawn on or to fear either the *belle comtesse* or the Pavillon Marsan. His influence with the king was employed rather beneficially for France than otherwise, his constitutional principles being opposed to the retrograde sentiments and impolitic measures of the " ultras " —a term first employed by M. Decazes to designate the " pure royalists."

"We have been tricked," said the Prince de Benevento to his colleagues, when the new cabinet was formed; "this is an intrigue that has been long in hand." He, however, secured a retiring pension of 100,000 *francs*, and a sinecure of importance in the king's household; while Louis was able, first preluding on the theme of the "inconceivable defection," to open his new Chambers with this gratifying announcement: the indemnity was reduced by his efforts from a thousand to seven hundred millions of *francs* (28,000,000 pounds sterling), to be paid in five years, 150,000 troops to remain in occupation

until the indemnity should be fully paid.   Gratifying indeed!   The first war tax was immediately
levied, and great difficulty experienced in collecting it.   Riots ensued, blood was shed, and "*À bas
les Bourbons!*" "*Vive Napoleon!*" were cries
which the utmost efforts of the police were unable
wholly to repress.   "The scaffold and the dun-
geon," says a French writer,* "could tell some
deplorable acts of reprisal at this time on the part
of the rulers whom the coalition of kings had
inflicted on a prostrate nation."

* Madame Junot.

CHAPTER XIX.

ARIE ANTOINETTE'S Château of St. Cloud had become, under the Napoleonic *régime*, a truly palatial residence. A handsome theatre had been erected, and some fine *salons* added to the old château; while the whole had been very richly redecorated, but in excellent taste, and sumptuously furnished. Louis XVIII. from his youth had loved splendour and luxury in his surroundings almost as much as from the same early period he had loved to indulge in the pleasures (as gluttony is termed) of the table. He was therefore delighted, when he paid his first visit to St. Cloud, to determine what portion of the château he preferred for his own exclusive residence, to find in the private apartments the same happy combination of magnificence, elegance, and comfort, so suited to his

self-indulgent and luxurious habits, as, with un-
looked-for satisfaction, he had succeeded to at the
Tuileries.

He was under the delusion that, besides being
of more illustrious descent than any other human
being, — for he scarcely deemed even his brother
and nephews quite his equals in that respect,— he
surpassed all men in natural endowments, both
intellectual and personal; and, as a matter of
course, in the profundity of his learning, as well
as worldly wisdom and general knowledge. He
piqued himself no less on the perfection of his
taste, which in early years had been guided by
that of his reputed mistress, Madame de Balby,
the lady who burnt the furniture of the apartments he had prepared for her, because of its
want of harmony and proper proportions. The
embellishments of his favourite château and domain of Brunoy were completed according to her
designs or suggestions; and, though there may
have been exaggeration in the praises bestowed
on them, Brunoy was regarded on the whole as
a model of what perfection of taste, with total
disregard of cost, can effect.

When, therefore, at St. Cloud, Louis XVIII.
was graciously pleased to accord the "usurper"
the possession of a modicum of that perfect taste
of which he believed himself to have a supera-
bundance, it must be admitted that it was praise
indeed. And this praise was fully echoed by all

who were privileged to see the embellishments
and luxurious arrangements that had called forth
the unwilling compliment.

But it was not only in the palace, but in the
park and grounds of St. Cloud, that the master's improving hand was visible. They had been
much enlarged, and laid out in less formal style.
The water-works, too, had been arranged on a
much improved system, and both the volume of
water and the height of the principal jets increased — glittering drops falling in a shower, or
in feathery spray, varying their former monotony.

These fountains when in full play had always
been an attractive sight. But agitating recent
events had so fully occupied the attention of both
people and rulers that some months had elapsed
since they were announced, as formerly, to play
at stated intervals. The Parisians seemed to
have given up their customary Sunday jaunt to
St. Cloud; and the fountains, continuing to send
forth no water, were in a fair way of being forgotten.

Paris, however, was full of English and other
visitors, of whom a very considerable sprinkling,
though possessing what was something less perhaps of a *passe-partout* then than now, a well-filled
purse, had not the *entrée* to the *salons* of the *élite*,
English or foreign. Lord and Lady Castlereagh
and Lord Stewart were supposed to keep open
house, though all were excluded except the exclu-

sives.   Then there were Lady Malmesbury's and
the Duchess of Wellington's receptions, which,
like other English *salons*, looked very brilliant and
gay when crowded with richly dressed women,
military officers, and diplomatists.   But the fine
dresses and uniforms are said to have been the
gayest part of the entertainment.

The few French ladies whom curiosity attracted
to these exclusive gatherings pronounced them
dull, inexpressibly dull.   The men were said to
congregate in groups to discuss public affairs.
The ladies were left to criticise each other, or, at
best, to laugh at French fashions, as the French
laughed at the English, their straw hats, their
green veils, and silk spencers, which they ended
by adopting.   They modified them, certainly, and
thus they were readopted by the English as a
caprice of *la mode française.*

Those unfortunate individuals who were a step
or two too low on the social ladder to obtain an
introduction to this dull but distinguished circle,
ventured, just as cats are permitted to look at
kings, to get a view of the sovereigns and mag-
nates of Europe at the theatres.   It appears that
on reassembling in Paris at the second restoration
they did not, as on the first occasion, enter much
into general society, but were more frequently to
be met with at the Opéra and other public places.
However, visitors who were not of the *crême de la
crême* of the *beau monde,* but merely *la crême des*

honnêtes gens, after having had, as they said, "a good look at the royalties," began to seek other amusements.

"When would the fountains of St. Cloud play again?" some inquired. None could tell. They had last played on the 21st of March to greet the emperor on his return. It was reported too, and found credence with many, that when the waters were then turned on they leaped from the fountains in a most unusual way, and with a sort of loud, long shriek that sounded to the ears of all present like "*Vive l'empereur!*" The water had been turned on since to greet "the Inevitable," but the fountains obstinately refused to send forth a drop of it. The reason why, nobody knew, though perhaps many could give a good guess. But they were soon to be tried again, and a *fête*, or a fair, at St. Cloud was talked of.

This was disappointing; for, confessedly, sight-seers found a dearth of amusement. They had visited the encampments, and they sometimes witnessed threatening collisions between French soldiers and foreign troops. They had probably taken the opportunity of seeing the plain of Waterloo, as depicted in an opera ballet, and a moving incident of the battle vigorously danced. A Highland regiment, chosen, of course, for the picturesque costume, and a detachment of the old French guard danced together in token of their deep sympathy with a lovely young lady whose

betrothed had been slain in the fight, she meanwhile portraying the madness of despair in *pirou-
ettes* and *entrechats*.

Most English visitors doubtless had made a
point of seeing Talma as Oreste in "*Andromaque*,"
which he played when Kemble returned Talma's
visit to England. The French tragedian then
gave a splendid supper, at which all the celebrities
of the French stage, and the *élite* of the artistic
and dramatic world, were assembled to do honour
to the great English actor.

Of course they had also seen the play of
"*Jeanne d'Arc*," in which their nation was so
vigorously denounced, and the denunciations and
political allusions as vigorously applauded. Lafond, who played Talbot, the English commander,
is said to have greatly enjoyed the storm of wrath
which his energetic performance brought down on
the personage he represented ; the public, with
whom he was a favourite, endeavouring at the
same time, by alternating "*À bas Talbot !*" with
"*Vive Lafond !*" to separate the actor from any
share in it. "Jeanne" was a great part with the
tragic actress Mdlle. Duchesnoy, whose alarming
ugliness startled those who saw her for the first
time. But, like Lekain, her powerful acting
overcame the disadvantages of personal unattrac-
tiveness. She commanded attention from the
moment she began to speak, and the entire sympathy of the audience soon followed.

Then there was Mdlle. Mars, whose face was as beautiful as that of Mdlle. Duchesnoy was plain, and whose fame equalled that of the tragic lady in the higher walk of comedy. They were the Siddons and Jordan of the French stage, the latter having a sort of political popularity super-added to her professional one, that of her amusingly persistent Bonapartism. As Louis XVIII. was, of course, in his own opinion, one of the greatest wits of the day, as well as one of the most gallant of mankind, he was not displeased to hear of the *spirituelles saillies* of a pretty woman.

She was, however, sufficiently astute to refrain from aiming her sometimes stinging *coups d'épingle* at the king; she cast them at his surroundings, and this Louis did not object to, for amongst his many great qualities he possessed a fair share of *malice*. It was customary with his first breakfast, of coffee and fifteen *côtelettes au jus*, to serve the daily dish of scandal and *bons mots*, diligently collected and invitingly prepared for him by his able *chef* the Minister of Police, who, by means of his numerous agents, may be said to have been ubiquitous so far as France was concerned. If from this dainty dish Louis chanced to pick out any piquant *jeu d'esprit* aimed at the *ultras* of the Pavillon Marsan, with whom he and his favourite minister were rarely in agreement, he took a secret pleasure in directing M. Decazes to see that it failed not to reach its address.

But if Mdlle. Mars, in virtue of her wit and beauty, was allowed unmolested to proclaim herself a Bonapartist, Louis, who professed himself a lover of justice, determined on recompensing the royalism of the pretty Mdlle. Bourgoin, a rival of the French Thalia, — not, however, in talent or beauty, but only in the advantage she had of being a few years younger. Gout and obesity prevented Louis XVIII. from frequenting the theatres ; but through the reports of his Minister of Police he knew all which that minister chose he should know of the sayings and doings of actors and actresses, both public and private.

Mdlle. Bourgoin, being reported devotedly royalist in her sentiments, and attractive in person, was accordingly summoned to appear in the royal presence ; and Louis put on the grand and gracious manner, so impressive, as he believed, and yet so encouraging to the timid and lower section of humanity, to receive the young lady when mysteriously introduced into his majesty's private cabinet or study. The first gentleman of the chamber placed a chair for her close to the king's, and remained in attendance ; but, by his royal master's order, with his back turned, and at a very respectful distance.

Taking Mademoiselle's hand, he raised it to his lips. Then smiling on her with great benignity, and assuming an air of as much gallantry as was possible under the unfavourable circumstances,

"Never," he said, with much emphasis, "until this day, have I so regretfully felt the weight of my twelve lustres." Mademoiselle smiled, and bowed her thanks for the implied compliment, but appears not to have ventured on replying. The king then began to question her about the parts in which she was most successful, and even attempted to rehearse a scene with her, he taking the lover's part.

Here her seriousness failed her. Louis's efforts to declaim the language of love in impassioned tones, instead of making the impression on the young lady it should have made, inspiring her with corresponding fervour, produced only an irrepressible fit of merry laughter. Notwithstanding this unmindfulness of the presence of the descendant of Saint Louis, the king paid her many compliments. Yet he was secretly vexed perhaps. For after having sufficiently, as it appeared to him, played the gallant, he put an end to the interview with the following quotation, which can scarcely be considered gracious or gallant*: "The best of company must part at last, said Dagobert to his dogs. (*Il n'est si bonne compagnie que ne se quitte enfin, disait Dagobert à ses chiens.*)"

But on the following morning a very handsome carriage drawn by a pair of fine bays drove up to the house where the lady resided. The first gen-

* *Mémoires d'un bourgeois de Paris.*

tleman-in-waiting, who had been present at the interview with his back turned, stepped out of the carriage.   He was the bearer of a complimentary message from his sacred majesty to Mdlle. Bourgoin, with a request that as a memento of their interview she would accept the present he sent her.   It was the carriage and horses in which the king's messenger had arrived ; also an elegant dressing-case with fittings in silver gilt, together with a sum of 30,000 *francs*.

This is considered to have been a solitary instance of gallantry and generosity on the part of Louis XVIII. towards a popular actress ; though whether intended as a tribute to her beauty and talent, or to the very pronounced royalist sentiments she professed in opposition to those of the greater actress, does not appear.   At all events, Mdlle. Bourgoin made no secret of the conquest she naturally supposed she had made on receipt of such valuable presents.

She walked for some days with a statelier step, and assumed a more queenly air, as became a lady wooed by a king.   And such a king !   "*Ce gros goutteux !* and must he, too, have his mistresses ?" exclaimed one of Mademoiselle's rejected lovers, as he indignantly resented the altered demeanour of the lady of his affections.   But, alas ! no first gentleman of the chamber was ever again despatched to carry presents and compliments to Mdlle. Bourgoin, or to summon her to another interview with her royal lover. The *belle* Comtesse du Cayla had heard of the visit of the royalist actress, and had ventured on a little witty badinage at her next morning visit. Louis received it very kindly. He liked to be thought a terrible fellow where ladies' hearts were concerned. But the lively countess conveyed the news to the austere duchess, who counted her beads, said a paternoster, and looked grave, very grave, by way of reproof, when next she saw that gay Lothario her royal uncle.

But she neither looked grave nor reproachfully when, at about the same time as he sent his presents to the pretty Mdlle. Bourgoin, he refused even to listen to a kneeling woman's appeal for mercy. A pitying friend had brought the wife of Général Mouton-Duvernet to the palace, vainly hoping that her heartrending agony might move the king to commute the general's sentence, and to be satisfied with banishment. His great soul, however, disdains the weakness of tempering with mercy what to his warped mental vision looks like justice. When wheeled along the gallery his eye rests on the unwelcome vision of a suppliant, and he screams in his impotent rage, " Take that woman away! take her out of my sight ! "

But let us throw a veil over these hideous assassinations. Leave the widow and the orphan to mourn their dead, and let us away to the *fêtes* with which these sanguinary scenes are so pleasantly varied. " I speak of *fêtes*," says a French writer

(Jouy), "in the circumstances in which we are now placed, because *fêtes* are given. And for those who undertake to depict the manners of the French, such a trait of character is of itself a picture."

But the *fête* of St. Cloud, with the fair and the fountains, to which both French and foreigners were looking forward with pleasing expectations, was not destined to take place. The king and his family and their partisans were afraid of the people. A superstitious feeling was gaining ground amongst them that something was about to happen that would drive "the Inevitable" and his relatives out of the country, and with the month of March and the flowers of spring, again and for good, bring back Napoleon. Some people asserted that he had never left the country, but was concealed, with his son and his wife, in some remote chambers at Fontainebleau, awaiting the completion of his plans.

Truly they who believed this could have known little of what was taking place in the world, and it appears they really did know very, very little beyond the fact that the nation was brought to the brink of ruin and was again under the sway of a hated dynasty. Any story then, if it promised relief from the "*gros goutteux*" and taxation, if it did not exactly obtain perfect credence, gave rise to hope that it might prove true.

As the objections to a *fête* at St. Cloud grew more formidable in the royal eyes the more they

were examined, a people's *fête* at Tivoli was substituted for it. There was to be a balloon ascent,
a great attraction, rendered still more attractive
by the fact of a young lady being the aeronaut ;
this was Mdlle. Garnerin, whose father had revived
Blanchard's idea of the parachute. She made the
ascent from the Tivoli gardens in a balloon, to
which a car with a parachute was attached. The
cords were to be cut at a given signal, and the
descent made with the parachute.

The young lady was dressed — one is almost
tempted to say inappropriately — in filmy white
muslin, so that a fleecy cloud seemed to envelop
her almost ere she had fairly quitted *terra firma*
for the region of clouds. A bunch of lilies in the
bosom of her dress and a wreath of them on her
head completed her aerial *toilette*. She carried in
her hand a small white flag, which she waved to
and fro as, amidst the acclamations of the thousands assembled to witness the ascent, she began
to soar aloft. But she had not soared far — little
more than a hundred yards or so, though the
height is described as "prodigious" — when the
affrighted spectators became alarmed for her
safety.

They urged and entreated, as with anxious
upturned eyes they watched her still ascending,
a thin white cloud partly veiling her from view,
that the signal (three rockets) for separating the
car from the balloon should be given. To ease

the minds of the people this was done ; but, to
their horror, the lady in the clouds heeded it not.
Upward still she soared. The alarm became
general. " She must have fainted ! "   " She is
afraid to separate the car from the balloon ! "
cried some.   " Ah! where will that infernal
machine carry her ? " screamed others.

Suddenly she emerges from the mist that had
momentarily concealed her from sight, and it is
perceived that the cords are cut and her frail bark
launched into space.   A thrill of terror rushes
through every breast ; a cry of alarm echoes
through that anxiously upward-gazing throng.
But at the same moment the parachute expands,
and the intrepid young aeronaut very leisurely
descends, so leisurely that she seems loth to quit
the aerial regions, and to return to *terra firma*
with regret.

"In the fulsome phraseology revived by the
Restoration," says the French writer before
named, " his sacred majesty most graciously
deigned to reward the courageous Mademoiselle
Garnerin by according her the high honour of
a presentation to him."   He received her with his
usual gracious senile simper, told her her beauty
equalled her courage, did her the further immense
favour of inflicting on her the penance of kissing
his gouty green-gloved hand, and as she knelt to
do so he quoted a line or two of Latin, probably
in one sense untranslatable, as the quotations of

this depraved-minded man addressed to ladies often were, then condescendingly waved her an adieu.

However flattering this may have been to Mdlle. Garnerin, yet it appears she had hoped that her friends would rather have obtained for her a presentation to the Duchesse d'Angoulême. The duchess, however, declined to receive her. "She did not patronise such pursuits." What, indeed, did she patronise? Certainly not art or literature. She resembled her mother in that, also in being no musician; though, unlike her, she forbore to exhibit her "royally bad" performances in public. The Duchesse d'Angoulême patronised only priestcraft, and art, so far as it was connected with the designing of embroidery for priestly vestments.

CHAPTER XX.

Matrimonial Proposals. — Throwing the Handkerchief. — The English Wife and Family. — Preparing to Receive the Bride. — The Glorious 2d of May. — The Emperor and His Generals. — Very Sorry; but It Cannot Be. — Going to Prayers. — " Peace on Earth and Mercy Mild." — The Saints and the Sinners. — Dignity Compromised. — A Hue and Cry. — A Fruitless Search. — Madame de La Valette. — The Gallant English Officers. — "Are You, Then, Athirst for His Blood?"

VERY strenuous efforts had been made by Louis XVIII. while in exile to obtain a royal bride for the Duc de Berry; but the prospect of a Bourbon restoration seemed, until 1812 or 1813, so very unlikely an event that Louis's matrimonial proposals on his nephew's behalf were invariably declined. The European courts were unwilling to give umbrage to Napoleon for the sake of an alliance that brought with it no sort of advantage, political or otherwise.

The Duc de Berry lived in exile a very dissipated life, as on returning to France he continued to do, squandering such small means as he possessed, and getting into debt as deeply as the tradespeople whom he honoured with his patronage allowed him. That he was already married in left-handed fashion would of course have been no obstacle to a royal marriage, had he otherwise been an eligible *parti*. But with Louis XVIII. on the throne of France, it became the duty of his younger nephew to perpetuate the royal line, and most of the European courts then had a princess to offer.

The double question of birth and religion disposed at once of the Russian alliance, though the duke was less punctilious on those points than his elders. Louis would have preferred the Princess Amelia of Saxony. "She was worthy," he said, "to wear a crown — even the crown of France." But unfortunately she was in delicate health. Austria offered an archduchess, a sister of Maria Louisa — a marriage that would have made Berry the brother-in-law of the "usurper." From such a connection the whole family naturally recoiled with pious horror, and the handkerchief at last fell at the feet of the Princesse Marie Caroline of Naples.

"I know instinctively," said the king, "that she will please France. She is a Bourbon, one of ourselves. I choose her then as my second beloved niece. Without having seen her, I know that she has many excellent qualities, that she is graceful, charming, talented, and devotedly attached to her ancient race." This important preliminary settled, "the great Blacas," as M. de Jaucourt calls him, prepared his travelling-carriages and again set forth for Italy; now to claim a bride, and to arrange the terms of a marriage instead of a concordat. He had but lately returned from Rome, when the king created him a duke.

The Duc de Berry meanwhile had his own private arrangements to see to. His English wife, Miss or Mrs. Amy Brown, was in Paris with his son and two daughters. He appears to have been very anxious about them, and doubtless they were amply provided for. * The public announcement of his approaching marriage was received with boundless joy by the royalists, with expressions of discontent by the rest of the nation. There were complaints of the waste of the public money in the extravagance of the preparations, at a time, too, when the people were so heavily burdened with an oppressive war tax and the support of a foreign army.

But murmurs and remonstrances of that kind were not likely to be heeded. The preparations to receive the bride in old *régime* fashion, both in Paris and at Fontainebleau, were continued with

* A paragraph in a London journal of very recent date mentioned the death of Thomas Brown at Nantes, in his 78th year. It stated that " he was one of the three children of the Duc de Berry and an English woman named Amy Brown. The two daughters were created countesses by Charles X., but he desired that the son should be inscribed on the Civil Register under the name simply of Thomas Brown. Amply provided for, as far as worldly goods were concerned, he led a tranquil and retired life in a provincial town, never meddling in politics, or in any way courting notoriety."

much alacrity. Her household was appointed, magnificent presents of diamonds employed the court jewellers, and the bridal carriages, lavishly ornamented, were nearly completed. The royal bridegroom's income of a million of *francs* was augmented ; and generally no expense was to be spared to celebrate the auspicious event with fitting splendour. The Parisians had therefore this consolation in the midst of their trouble, and to many no doubt it sensibly diminished the burden — the certainty of a fortnight of unceasing gaiety and festivity.

Balls, public and private, every night ; general illuminations ; free entrance to the theatres, with special appearance of the royalties ; picturesque scenes on the Seine, and tournaments in the gardens ; grand military spectacles in the Champ de Mars, and reviews of troops, French and foreign. That the latter for so signal an occasion might, without any laceration of their feelings as conquerors, be impressed into the service of the conquered, was unanimously conceded by their commanders. Such, then, was a portion of the programme for the celebration of the forthcoming great national event.

Of course, no day for the ceremony could then be precisely fixed. Preparations were making at Naples, with the leisurely speed of the Italians, for the despatch of the bride. The journey in ·those days was also an affair of time, especially for a princess whom a complimentary demonstration awaited at every town on her route. The king accordingly availed himself of this delay to allow his loving subjects to get up an ovation in his own honour — to celebrate, in fact, the glorious 2d of May, the anniversary of his first entry into Paris.

When this was arranged, Sir Robert Wilson, Colonel Hutchinson, and another officer were on their trial before the judges of the High Court of Justice for complicity in a plot against the state. In other words, they were arraigned for aiding in defrauding the guillotine of a victim, Général de La Valette, condemned by the Court of Assizes to an ignominious death. Immediately on the flight of the king, the general (as already mentioned) resumed his former office of Director of the Posts, and despatched the news of the emperor's return to all the departments of France. After the disastrous battle of Waterloo he and Général de La Bédoyère, with other officers, accompanied Napoleon to Rochefort, where they would have embarked with him for America.

Two vessels had been placed at the emperor's disposal by the provisional government. But the infamous Fouché, in close communication with the allies, saw in the concession of these vessels the means of ensnaring their prey; for they seemed to shrink from actually laying hands on him. English ships blockaded the port; to pass out, a safe-conduct was needed. It was applied for, but the Duke of Wellington refused it. When the emperor went on board the English ship, La Bédoyère and La Valette were not permitted to embark with him. The former had already been judicially assassinated, and the latter, now escaped, sentenced to death before even he was arrested.

He appeared before the court on the 20th of November; his sentence being more ignominious than La Bédoyère's, because, in addition to "plotting against the head of the state," he was accused of "usurpation of public functions under the royal government." The sentence was appealed against; but the Court of Cassation confirmed it. The object, however, was to gain time, and during the month that intervened great efforts were vainly made to obtain a remission of the sentence of death. His own urgent request to the king was that, "as a soldier who had served his country, he might be spared the disgrace of the guillotine, and his majesty graciously order that he should be shot."

The court of Bavaria very persistently addressed the king in his favour, at which the amiable duchess was exceedingly indignant, Bavaria being but a second-rate, perhaps only a third-rate, Power. The Emperor of Austria pleaded also, and made the remission of the general's sentence a personal favour to himself.

Louis was very sorry, of course. But "this man was not less guilty than Maréchal Ney, Général de La Bédoyère, and some others he named. He had not spared them. Justice must take its course."

The general seems to have had troops of friends, and among them was Maréchal Marmont. His treachery had been of so much service to the Bourbon cause that he might surely claim to be heard when he pleaded. The Duchesse d'Angoulême had positively refused to receive the Comtesse de La Valette, and orders were given to attendants not to admit her to the palace. Marmont, nevertheless, accompanied her thither. She passed in with him, and was placed in the gallery through which the duchess went to the chapel to hear mass.

She wore deep mourning; and as the duchess approached she knelt before her, sobbing, but unable to utter a word. Marmont stood beside her. He states that the duchess, with a movement of impatience, on seeing Madame de La Valette, momentarily turned towards her; but with a look expressive of more intense hatred and disgust than he could have believed a human countenance capable of assuming. He says he was startled by it. She then passed on, to say her prayers — to thank God probably that she was not so weak as other women were, or even as some men. Intercession then was useless. " An

example is necessary," said the Pavillon Marsan
coterie, as though no other blood had been shed.

The execution was to take place on Christmas
Day! — a worthy celebration, certainly, of the
festival of peace on earth and good-will towards
all men. At about four o'clock on Christmas eve,
just when a cold and cheerless day was closing in,
and the gloomy shadows of night were gathering
over dimly lighted Paris, Madame de La Valette,
accompanied by her daughter, a girl of twelve
years, and a female servant, arrived in a sedan
chair, as she had done on previous occasions, at
the prison of the Conciergerie. She was much
wrapped up in furs, and wore the large flapping
hat which the English ladies had introduced, and,
besides, was thickly veiled. She and her daughter
were admitted to the prisoner's cell; and, as husband and wife were to take their final leave of
each other, they were left with their child alone
for awhile, the servant remaining at the door.

Shortly after, she leaves the prison sobbing
violently, her veil and her handkerchief concealing
her face, and scarcely prevented from falling, though
supported on either side by her servant and child.
The gaolers are moved to pity. The turnkey
waits a few minutes ere he returns to his prisoner,
to allow him to overcome the state of emotion in
which, after such a parting, he expects to find him.
But on opening the door of his cell, what is his
amazement — real or feigned (for one or more

must have been in the secret) — Madame de La
Valette stands, transfixed, as it were, before him.
She wears her husband's clothing, but offers no
explanation. She is motionless, silent, rigid ; her
eyes, with a stony stare of terror, gazing on the
door. Her reason is gone, poor victim !

A hue and cry is immediately raised. What a
commotion it creates at the Tuileries among the
pious, who are at their Christmas eve devotions,
when, like a thunderbolt in their ears, comes the
announcement : "Général de La Valette has
escaped !" Louis XVIII. and his *chère amie, en
tête-à-tête*, are discussing the forthcoming marriage. "Again, then," says the fair countess,
"the now dreary *salons* of the Tuileries are to
resound with mirth and laughter !" And the
king replies that all balls, concerts, theatricals,
and other gaieties of the revived court will belong
to the department of the future young Duchesse
de Berry. He is all good humour this evening,
full of the milk of human kindness. He has
resolved that, until the marriage festivities are
ended, there shall be no more executions after La
Valette's head has fallen. He feels as benignant
as if he had granted another general amnesty.

He has just placed an ample pinch of snuff, as
is customary with him, on the countess's ivory
shoulder, whence he removes it in sundry small
pinches, or, occasionally leaning towards her, in-
hales it. At that moment, with an unceremoni-

ousness unusual with him, and, indeed, never permitted by his royal master, M. Decazes enters the apartment. He has an affrighted air. The king looks daggers. The countess affects the superb and shakes the snuff from her shoulder, which makes the king sneeze and greatly compromises his dignity.

M. Decazes is now Comte Decazes. The king is looking out for a suitable wife for him. He has a fine estate or two, possesses his majesty's full confidence, and by and by he will be Duc Decazes. Still there are times and seasons, as he knows, when even he must not intrude. And for the world he would not do so. " But " — he is beginning to apologise, when the king, perceiving the pallor of his countenance, relents.

" *Mon enfant,*" he says (he now always addresses Decazes as " my child," or " my dear child ") — " *mon enfant,* what has happened to bring you here at this hour ? "

" Sire, Général de La Valette has escaped," he exclaims, in a tone that seems to say, " Pray pardon me," for he is Minister of Police, be it remembered.

" Général de La Valette escaped ! " echoes Louis, and reëchoes Madame du Cayla.

M. Decazes then relates particulars, and adds that the telegraph has been set to work, a watch placed at all the barriers, and orders issued to search the houses of the general's friends. The

king commends his favourite's zeal, and M. Decazes departs, to take such further steps to trace
or retake the criminal as may in his wisdom seem
good.

No sooner had the door closed on M. Decazes
than the countess began, " If Fouché had been
Minister of P——" The king raised his hand
deprecatingly. " Madame," he said, " has *her* department, the Minister of Police has *his*, and both
fulfil their duties admirably." Madame was about
to insist that M. Decazes was a Jacobin, and probably a party to the general's escape ; that he
alienated the affections of the royalists from their
sovereign, and that the sovereign himself seemed
inclined to pass over to the enemy's camp. But
the king began to doze. Their interview had
lasted longer than usual. When, therefore, he
again for a moment opened his drowsy eyes, his
fair friend wished him a good night and pleasant
dreams ; then withdrew to ascertain how the Comte
d'Artois and the duchess bore their disappointment.

The measures taken by M. Decazes for
La Valette's rearrest proved utterly unavailing.
Wherever the telegraph announced his escape, acclamations and *vivas* attested the delight of the
people. The joy was as general as when, using
the telegraph himself, he sent the news of the
emperor's arrival to every part of France. But
he was still in Paris. On leaving the prison a

carriage awaited him on the quay. It was driven by a lady, disguised, the Princesse de Vaudemont, who conducted him to a place of safety and concealed him until he could cross the frontier. Several times her house was searched, but as vainly as the houses of other friends. Yet the disguise he escaped in was burnt there, and through her influence he was conveyed to the frontier of Holland by Sir Robert Wilson, Captain Hutchinson, and another officer, to all of whom he was a stranger.

Général de La Valette wore the uniform of an English quartermaster-general when the above-named officers openly drove him through Paris. He was indebted to the princess for the carrying out of the skilfully arranged plot to which he owed his escape. She had so thoroughly taken her precautions that the only failure feared was in the important part assigned to his wife. She herself doubted that she would have sufficient nerve to carry her through it. At first she hesitated to undertake it; then refused. But the sterner-minded princess prevailed, by showing her that it was her duty, and almost commanding her to do it, leaving the rest to her.

Madame de La Valette never recovered from the shock her reason sustained under the excessive terror she experienced while contributing to her husband's escape. It is owing to this melancholy circumstance probably that the general (in his Memoirs) has ascribed to his wife the sole credit of saving him from an ignominious end. Perhaps, too, the princess might not have desired that the active part she took in the plot should be openly avowed. Its perfect success, however, boldly and skilfully as she laid her plans, really depended on Madame de La Valette, who nerved herself to do what from natural timidity she shrank from, and became so sadly the victim instead of a participator in the joy of its happy results. On leaving France, Général de La Valette retired to Bavaria, and after five years of this self-banishment was pardoned.

The trial of his three English deliverers naturally excited great general interest. The court was filled with ladies. Lady Grantham, the Marchioness of Conyngham, Lady Francis Cole, the Countess of Glengall, and many of the *élite* of the English circle, were present; and amongst other notabilities, Madame Jérôme Bonaparte (Mrs. or Miss Patterson). She is described as being then very pretty, not particularly graceful; more lively than, considering her position, some persons thought she ought to be, and with manners *très prononcées*, which rather shocked the shy English ladies of that day.

The gallant Sir Robert — who had a spice of romance in his character — was acquitted, with, of course, his equally gallant companions. The procureur-général, says a writer of the time, with

all his rabid eloquence, failed to impart to an act
of humanity the semblance of a capital crime.
But they were ordered to pay the expenses of the
procès, and some accounts state that they were
under arrest for three months for breach of military discipline.

The king not only effected cheerfully to accept
the result of the trial, but declared that the English officers had really done him a service, by
releasing him from the embarrassing position in
which he was placed towards those of his allies
who had solicited the guilty general's pardon.
"La Valette had escaped, and he was glad of it."
He even gave countenance to the rumour, set
afloat by "royalists more royalist than the king,"
that he and his Minister of Police facilitated the
escape. Yet they did not fail to dismiss and
severely punish the head gaoler.

The Duchesse d'Angoulême was so vehement
in the expression of her rage at the escape of the
prisoner, and her intense dissatisfaction with the
result of the trial of its abettors, that Louis XVIII.,
who certainly could not be called a humane man,
thus sternly checked his wrathful niece, " Are you,
then, athirst for his blood ? "

CHAPTER XXI.

ERHAPS the people were put into good
humour by the report, emanating, as
supposed, from the ultra-royalists to
rouse the less ardent of their party, that the king,
led astray by his favourite, the Minister of Police,
was fast degenerating into liberalism. The Minister, through his numerous staff of secret agents,
may have circulated this report. A little popularity for himself and a semblance of enthusiasm
for the king were needed for the due celebration
of the anniversary of the return of "the Inevitable " to his longing people on the memorable
2d of May. " How could it otherwise have
happened," asks a cynical writer, "that so many
of the people, to commemorate that unhappy event,

devoted the livelong day to pleasure, instead of fasting in sackcloth and ashes ?" However, so it happened ; and from the break of dawn, when a hundred guns announced the birth of the auspicious day, Paris was a scene, if not of pleasure, at least of noisy revelry. Louis himself was satisfied, and his Minister equally so.

But at the daily interview Louis learned from the countess that the immaculates of the Pavillon Marsan were far from being satisfied.

" What," he inquired, " are their reasons, madame ?"

" Sire, an illustrious lady and her uncle think that the day should have been marked by more solemnity."

" Madame, I beg to remind you of the *Te Deum* in all the churches ; also at the royal chapel, which a little gout that sometimes troubles me did not allow me to attend. Her royal highness and my august brother and nephews doubtless did so. And yourself, madame ?"

" Oh, certainly, Sire. I am, as your majesty knows, a royalist."

" And the king, madame ?"

" Ah, Sire !"

" The king is a Jacobin, is not he, madame ?"

" Sire, I should not dare to use that term, though there are bold tongues that do not shrink from it ; and if I may venture, without offending your majesty, to repeat what is said in pure royalist circles, it is asked, 'What, alas! will this lead to?'"

Louis was a little offended. But although, as he said, this lady and he had frequent quarrels, — she affecting ultra principles, while, in fact, she was a liberal, — yet her soft, insinuating voice and the charm of her gentle manners had so soothing an effect on him that his anger with her was very different from that which he felt when other people provoked him. To her remark, "What, alas! will this lead to?" he replied:

"Madame, the festive occasion we first were speaking of will lead to another of equal importance. The *fêtes* and national rejoicings will, however, be of longer duration. The court and the people will participate in them; and none, I firmly believe, madame, will find more enjoyment in them than yourself." The lady smiled on her royal *cher ami*, and bowed her assent to his words. For it was she who had urged him to revive the gaieties of the old court of France, as the young *noblesse* were dying of *ennui*.

The embroidery designs for the coat which the king had ordered, to do honour to the royal marriage, were submitted to her for approval before they were put in hand. The coat was of velvet, *bleu du roi*, his favourite colour, embroidered in white silk mixed with seed pearls. A pair of half boots of velvet — colour not named — lightly embroidered, were also prepared for the occasion.

The famous " Regent " diamond, which had glit-
tered for twelve years in Napoleon's sword-hilt, was
now transferred to Louis's new plumed hat; and
the somewhat less lustrous " Sancy," which the
emperor occasionally wore in his hat, now decorated the king's sword. These, and some ample
garments of white satin with diamond buckles,
were all prepared and pac ced for early despatch
to Fontainebleau, and Louis flattered himself that
when arrayed in his wedding suit he should far
outshine all the rest of the company.

The Princesse Marie Caroline Ferdinande was
married by proxy at Naples, in that same palace
where, but a twelvemonth before, the unfortunate
Joachim Murat reigned. The Duc de Blacas-
d'Aulps represented the bridegroom. On the
30th of May the princess landed at Marseilles,
and was received by the Duc d'Avray, the Duchesse de Reggio, and two other ladies. Etiquette
did not permit the Duc de Berry to proceed
thither in person. He, however, had the gallantry
to be anxious to go to Naples and bring the bride
thence to France himself; and he wrote to the
princess to express his regret that he could not do
so, being of course compelled, as he said, to submit to the decrees of their elders. However, what
was denied to the bridegroom was permitted to a
party of the younger *noblesse*, who accompanied
the ladies of the household to Marseilles to escort
the princess thence to Fontainebleau.

The duke was rather painfully doubtful of the effect his personal appearance and twenty years of seniority might have on a lively young lady of eighteen. He expressed as much in his letters, and spoke rather disparagingly of his personal endowments. In her replies she seemed desirous of putting him at ease on that matter; but she reproves him for writing too hastily, and says that, "greatly delighted though she was to read his letters, he had caused that pleasure to be delayed by the necessity she was under of studying his writing before she could read it. She hopes he will not think, because she mentions it, that she is difficult to please and inclined to scold, but his writing was not very legible, such was the fact."

Royalist accounts speak of the splendour with which, in all its details, this marriage was celebrated, as surpassing all preceding ones. Probably the marriage of Napoleon and Maria Louisa would not be included by a Bourbonite in the category of royal marriages; but there is no doubt that it far exceeded the Duc de Berry's in magnificence. In both instances the ceremonial observed was as nearly as possible the same as when Marie Leczinska was married to Louis XV., and Marie Antoinette to the dauphin, afterwards Louis XVI.

Two richly tapestried and decorated tents were erected in the forest. The royal family and attendant grand dignitaries assembled in one of them to await the arrival of the bride. Louis meanwhile, arrayed in his wedding garments and reposing in his easy chair, received the compliments of all present on the richness, yet chaste and elegant simplicity, of his dress, its exquisite taste, and extreme becomingness. He glanced at the countess, who was present, though she held no appointment in the new royal household. She was there because his sacred majesty willed it. And exceedingly handsome she looked in her rich dress of *rose Du Barry* brocade, antique point-lace, and pearls. Louis admired her almost as much as he admired himself.

But list! They hear the sound of coaches. It is the rumbling of the capacious and highly ornamented state carriages in which the young princess and her retinue travel the last stage of their journey. What a commotion her entry occasions amongst this pompous assemblage, who, in their eagerness to gratify curiosity, forget for the moment all the grand manners and formal etiquette observed on such courtly occasions. "We allowed our hearts to play their part in the bride's reception," says the Duc de Doudeauville, speaking in the name of Louis XVIII. But whether the sudden and unexpected departure from the prescribed forms was to be attributed to sentiment or curiosity, the utter upset of his very precise arrangements greatly chagrined the

Marquis de Dreux-Brézé, grand master of the ceremonies.

The Comte de Ségur, who filled the same post of honour during the empire, and, to Louis's amazement and indignation, applied to be reinstated in it when the restoration took place, had made some strange mistakes, it appears, when reviving the old *régime* etiquette in the imperial *salons*.   But here was a grand master born to the manner of these old-world ways, and fondly cherishing them as having their part in the halo of glory that illumined the throne of the Bourbon monarchy.   In his great zeal he had personally superintended every detail of the ceremony of the reception.   He had given explanations to the less well-informed when requested, and had taken the trouble to have the attendants thoroughly rehearsed in the duties which on this special occasion devolved on them.   The reward he naturally sought was that all should go smoothly, from scene the first to the end.

The bride, being a Bourbon, had been well initiated in the theory of the right divine, its sacred privileges, etc., and in that respect she was stanch.   But she was young and lively, and the restraints of etiquette bored her exceedingly. Before leaving Naples she had been thoroughly admonished, in order to tone down her rather exuberant spirits to a point of gravity consistent with the responsible position of a possible queen of France and the probable mother of its king. Everywhere on her journey from Marseilles — which occupied a fortnight — she had met with a sympathetic welcome ; and the honours that were paid her she received with a sort of gracious gaiety, which, while expressing her own delight, delighted others.

M. de Brézé had forwarded to Marseilles, for the information of the ladies of honour, a programme of the ceremonial of the bride's reception. On looking it over they agreed that it would be advisable to school the princess a little in the part she had to play in it. She might otherwise bend or bow, or kneel or partly kneel, at the wrong time, and be raised or partly raised, or paternally blessed, by the wrong persons.

When the *cortège* arrived at the Cross of St. Hérem, and her carriage drew up at the entrance of the tent of honour, the princess's countenance was perceived to be slightly serious. She was seized with doubts of her ability to walk with a slow and dignified *menuet-de-la-cour* sort of step to the centre of the tent, where somebody would be waiting to conduct her to somebody else. But no sooner was the carriage door opened, than, giving up her onerous duties apparently altogether, the fair young bride jumped lightly out, and, unmindful of the bowing, cringing groups in attendance around her, tripped into the tent unattended. This unexpected and unceremonious

appearance of the sprightly *ingénue* caused a
general sensation.   The bridegroom, by an irresistible impulse, it seems, sprang forward to meet
her, seized her hand, and kissed it.   Thus terrible
confusion ensued ; all the parts were changed,
and M. de Brézé was ready to sink into the earth
with shame and vexation.

It was the Comte d'Artois who should have
advanced with a dignified step and air, not have
rushed or sprung forward, to meet and welcome
the young lady and conduct her to the king;
before whom she should have kneeled.   His majesty should have graciously raised her, or, gout
not permitting, have bidden her raise herself,
embraced her, and delivered her up with a blessing to the Duc de Berry.   In his turn he should
have presented his bride to the Duc and Duchesse
d'Angoulême ; while others present, according to
their several degrees of rank, should have craved
the honour of paying their homage and laying
themselves at her feet.   Much more of this, and
no less impressive in character, was of course set
down in the programme.   But when the heart, as
the king said, claimed to share in it, there was an
end to all courtly proceedings, and the whole affair was conducted with a sort of *bourgeois* hilarity
distressing to witness in so august an assembly.

The gay young princess had imparted a little of
her own airy spirits to the prosy elderly circle, and
all were delighted.   Even the austere countenance

of the Duchesse d'Angoulême relaxed into the shadow of a smile. The Duc de Berry thought his bride charming, and, says the king, with his accustomed gallantry, he was not the only one of the family of that opinion.

A grand banquet was in course of preparation in the adjoining tent. But when about to repair to it, the princess was near spoiling his majesty's appetite, and throwing a gloom over the spirits of some others of the royal party whom her bright presence had made so unwontedly gay. She suddenly expressed her surprise and disappointment at the absence of her uncle and aunt D'Orléans. By the startled countenances of those around her, she perceived there was some indiscretion in her remark, though she knew not what it was. But as none ventured to reply to it, the king himself answered: "My dear child, his *serene* highness" (he was fond of emphasising that word) "and family are now in England."

The king intended his reply to be a full and final one to her question, and the princess was sufficiently acute and clever, for the time being, so to receive it. Thus the menaced interruption to the general harmony was warded off ; and as Louis proceeded with his dinner — which it appears was a long protracted, elaborate, and highly satisfactory one — the unwelcome image of the intriguing and mistrusted Duc d'Orléans gradually faded from his mental vision.

No receptions took place at the palace of Fontainebleau. That splendid royal residence, where both royal and imperial courts had given such magnificent *fêtes*, such grand hunting parties, and *fêtes champêtres*, in the woods, seemed to be avoided by the Bourbons. They shrank from it as though they shared the popular delusion that a Napoleon II. was growing up in some remote corner of that princely dwelling ; and for many a year to come no royal visitor entered it. The most meagre preparations only were made for resting beneath its roof a few hours, the day being too far advanced to return to Paris on the 14th.

Early on the morrow the royal party were on their way to the capital. The Comte de Chabrol, Prefect of the Seine, with the municipal authorities, was of course in waiting at the city gates to welcome the bride, to harangue the king, and generally to compliment and render homage in the name of the city of Paris. "M. le Préfet," replied the king, "you see me return accompanied by my children. You well know my paternal heart, and will therefore readily comprehend my happiness. To see that my faithful subjects participate in it gratifies me exceedingly."

On the 17th the marriage was solemnised at Notre-Dame with wondrous pomp, the number of crowned heads and other royal personages who attended it giving exceptional *éclat* to this ceremony, for which a musical mass, said to have been extremely impressive, was specially composed. Neither pains nor expense were spared to secure the acclamations of the fickle Parisians ; and little difficulty was there in accomplishing this object. For, though one day bitterly complaining of burdensome taxation, of the ignominious presence in their midst of a foreign army, far, very far, outnumbering their own, and of many things besides which displeased them, chief among which was "the Inevitable" and his family; the next, proclaim but a *fête*, an illumination, a gorgeous procession (if it was not an ecclesiastical one), a Tivoli ball, a balloon or two, or special theatrical representation, and all was changed.

When the procession of the bride and bridegroom passed through Paris, it was who should cry the loudest. "*Vive Henri Quatre*" and "*Charmante Gabrielle*" saluted them everywhere. One would have thought they were that celebrated pair of lovers in person. All who had any tapestry decorated with it the fronts of their houses ; those who had none hung out their curtains and carpets ; and when at night the general illumination made Paris all aglow with colour from the refulgent rays of myriads of many-coloured lamps, enthusiasm reached its highest pitch. Gathering in one vast crowd before and around the Tuileries, which was brilliantly lighted up, they vied with each other in raving their *vivas* for the king, for Madame la Duchesse and M. le Duc de Berry.

This, however, was a breach of etiquette. So near the royal palace they should have been content to gaze in ecstatic joy, to wave their hats, their handkerchiefs, or to express their feelings less noisily. It was on the present occasion inconveniently overwhelming, and was about to be suppressed, when the king, who thought it more prudent to encourage than to check sounds so unwonted, declared it to be his *bon plaisir* that the delirious joy of his faithful lieges should not be interrupted. "It is their hearts that speak," he said ; "and mine excuses them."

The newly married Duchesse de Berry was by no means beautiful. Though she was in her eighteenth year, her appearance and manners were those of a girl of fifteen. But she had a pleasing expression, an engaging smile, and merry laugh. She was of medium height, and her figure slight and graceful. Her education had been much neglected ; but this and the girlish petulance she at times exhibited were counterbalanced by her desire to cultivate the talents she possessed and to patronise the arts, and by her affability and the gaiety of her Southern temperament. She was passionately fond of pleasure. The court was therefore delighted with her, both the old and the new *noblesse* ; yet at first they regarded her more as a charming spoiled child than as a leader of the court society.

So much of a child was she that some ingenious

toys were made expressly to amuse her. The furniture of her dressing-room was also of a fanciful kind, the toilet-table, glass, and chair being all mounted in diamond-cut crystal, and having some concealed mechanism attached to them, which when wound up played two tunes each, for her amusement, probably, while dressing. On returning to the palace of the Élysée, the Duc de Berry's residence, after the ceremony at Notre-Dame, it being supposed she must feel both fatigued and agitated, she was left for awhile in her apartment alone, that she might rest and recover composure.

Time, more than sufficient for this purpose, it was thought, having elapsed, the Duc de Berry ventured to take advantage of his newly acquired privileges to enter the young bride's apartment. His astonishment was great indeed when he beheld his *petite duchesse* still wearing her grand court costume of white brocade embroidered in silver and diamonds, plumes on her head, and diamond coronet. Her train, which was six yards in length, and had been borne by six ladies of distinction, there being then a scarcity of royal princesses at the court of France, was twisted several times round her arm ; while she, humming a lively tune, was dancing gaily round the chairs and tables with a pet spaniel she had brought from Naples, and which she was holding up by his forepaws.*

* Private letters of 1816.

CHAPTER XXII.

ADAME la Duchesse de Berry began very soon to tire of her toys, and to prefer dancing at fancy balls to dancing with her dogs. The Duchesse d'Angoulême's title of Madame Royale was, however, now more than hitherto insisted on at court; probably to mark that her place there was above that of the aspiring young lady who sought to grasp the sceptre of queen of the revels and of *la mode*. The royal sisters-in-law were compared to Madame de Maintenon and the lively young Duchesse de Bourgogne, the mother of Louis XV. It was a comparison rather disparaging to the lady whose enemies gave her the *sobriquet* of the "*fausse prude*," for if she did not always approve of the duchess's escapades, she was much more tolerant of them, and often threw a veil over indiscretions which needed more veiling than those of the Duchesse de Berry.

Madame Royale had smiled almost benignantly at Fontainebleau on the girlish bride, whose youthful appearance was heightened by abundance of beautiful fair hair flowing in natural curls over her shoulders. She believed she saw in her a future saint, a child of plastic nature, to be moulded by her own and able Jesuit hands into a bright example of piety to the younger nobility. They, too generally well disposed, as she perceived with pain, towards a renewal of the gaieties which she would repress, strove earnestly for emancipation from the restraints of the formal etiquette of the old court which, with priestly rule, it was her aim to revive.

She was rather disconcerted, yet not wholly discouraged, by the ill success of her first attempts to check the disposition which the young duchess soon evinced to delight in the pomps and vanities of the world. Paris had not been so generally devoted to pleasure and dissipation for many a day as during the month following the royal marriage. This was an evil for which there was no remedy ; but, the nuptial festivities ended, Madame looked forward to exhorting, admonishing, and reproving with better effect. Inviting the duchess into her oratory, that the lesson, aided by its solemn surroundings, might be more impressive, Madame began to talk in serious tones of the evanescence of earthly pleasures. Pointing to more

enduring ones, she urged her to pursue the path
that led to them, keeping ever in view the promised reward, a heavenly crown, and fleeing, as she
would fly for her life, those pleasures of sense that
wrought the soul's perdition.*

This, with very much more of warning to flee
from the wrath to come, was — with the best
intentions, no doubt — pressed on the unwilling
ear of the pleasure-loving Duchesse de Berry
whenever opportunity occurred.   But this was not
often; for she was intent on enjoying the pleasures of the passing hour, and cared not to be saddened by her severe sister-in-law's homilies.   They
were to her, as the bigotry of the duchess was to
ladies of the court generally, a sort of wet blanket,
whose unpleasant contact she resolved to avoid;
therefore she complained to her husband.   He,
who approved all she did, and had modified to a
great extent the dissipated life he led before his
marriage, in order to devote himself to his charming bride and to share her tastes and amusements,
was immensely annoyed that so perfect a little
woman should be so harshly, as he considered,
taken to task; so he appealed to his father.

The reformed *roué*, like many others of the
dreary court, had fallen under the spell of the
light-hearted Italian girl, so soon become as thoroughly Parisian as though her adopted country
were her native one.   This, to many, was not the

* Private letters of 1816 and 1817.

least of either her charms or her merits, and, being
purposely made public, secured her much popularity. The Comte d'Artois, therefore, though
not disposed to reprove the young duchess for
taking the initiative in the organisation of court
balls, concerts, etc., as Madame Royale neglected
to do so, yet felt bound to join the latter in a
word of admonition concerning the *flânerie* of both
duchess and duke.

This gay pair, between whom there appears to
have been a strong attachment as well as sympathy in their tastes, rambled about Paris together; visited the *ateliers* of the painters in
vogue, Gérard, Girodet, the Vernets, etc., quite
in *bourgeois* fashion. Sometimes they went out
on foot, at others in a tiny open carriage driven by
the duke, but always unattended. They also frequented the *salons*, of which two or three were
reopened about the time of the marriage; but
desiring always that they might not be troubled
by any restraints of etiquette — that was to be
reserved for formal state occasions. At the *réunions* of the Russian Princess Bagration they
were frequently met with. The princess was the
wife of the Russian field-marshal of that name,
and was then a very beautiful woman. She was
one of the most brilliant stars of the constellation
of beauties that had shone at Vienna when the
sovereigns and princes of Europe were assembled
there, "amusing themselves *en vacances*," as the

Prince de Ligne said of the royal personages at the Congress.

The Emperor Alexander, when, as sometimes had happened,* he was faithless to mysticism and Madame de Krüdener, might not unfrequently be found in the splendid *salons* of the Hôtel Bagration in the Rue Mont Blanc (Chaussée d'Antin). But not only emperors, kings, and princes, distinguished generals, diplomatists, and statesmen were attracted thither by the charms of the gracious and graceful hostess ; the cordial welcome that awaited the *élite* of the literary and artistic world drew poets, painters, and musicians, and every writer of any eminence, to her receptions.

It was there that the talent of the young Italian composer and *pianiste*, Donizetti, was first made known to aristocratic Paris. Donizetti had just arrived from Italy, recommended to the princess, which was more fortunate for him than if he had been recommended to the patronage of the court. He was then scarce twenty years of age, and ex-

* In the autumn of 1815, when the Treaty of the Holy Alli ance had been proposed and signed. " Prince Metternich has been suspected of imagining this league offensive and defensive of the sovereigns against the people, he being the oracle whose lessons Madame de Krüdener repeated and covered with a veil of vague and mystic language." Yet it was written in pencil wholly by Alexander, and revised by Madame de Krüdener, who gave it its name of the " Sainte Alliance." The fit of transitory enthusiasm to which she owed her influence over the emperor gradually died out after leaving Paris.

ceedingly handsome. "His smile," said the Comtesse de Bassanville, "is that of hope, and the expression of his eyes reveals genius. His voice is divine; he sings as they sing in heaven; and he is so good and so amiable that none can know him and fail to love him."

The Princess Bagration had good reason to be proud of her *protégé*, for he was a *protégé* whose brilliant talent needed no patron. But she presented il Signor Gaetano Donizetti to all her friends, predicting as she did so that the future composer of "*Lucia di Lammermoor*," "*Lucrezia Borgia*," "*La Favorita*," "*La Fille du Régiment*," etc., would surely become a great *artiste ;* and a great *artiste* he became. But, alas! this youth, so full of genius, and destined to achieve honours, wealth, and fame, was destined also to lose the light of reason, and at a comparatively early age to end his days in a madhouse.

Among English visitors of distinction and literary fame who assiduously visited at the Hôtel Bagration at this time (1816 and 1817), Lord Byron may be named, though he does not appear to have been a favourite either in English or foreign society. The French thought him "cold and haughty, wrapped up in self, often assuming for effect an inspired air; and if perchance a few civil words escaped his mocking lips, appearing to expect that the fortunate individual to whom they were addressed should be overwhelmed with delight at the honour done him." It was, however, admitted that, although lame, his lameness was not ungraceful, and that he might have been a charming cavalier had he but condescended to be one.

M. de Châteaubriand, in his amazing vanity, was jealous beyond measure of the poet. Any praise bestowed on his works irritated him greatly; for he considered it as depriving him of a portion of his fame to bestow it on a writer unworthy to be ranked with the author of the " *Génie du Christianisme.*" Byron, however, was but one among many whose fame displeased M. de Châteaubriand, and was resented by him as though it were a personal affront.

But it was especially at the *soirées intimes* that the Duc and Duchesse de Berry were allowed to enjoy themselves as simple mortals. It was necessary, however, that the princess should issue a stringent order that her royal guests were not to be recognised; otherwise some among those who sought the privilege of being admitted would doubtless have availed themselves of an opportunity of falling at their feet and worshipping. This might have pleased Madame Royale; but the aim of the younger lady was not to inspire the faithful with awe by her presence, but to receive every one graciously, and when she departed to leave a trace of joyousness behind her; and this she contrived to do in a perfectly natural manner, being amiable, charitable, and conciliatory.

But, although she won golden opinions from all conditions and parties, — some of the factions into which the community was divided beginning to fancy that the duke, her husband, the modern Henri IV., guided by so wise and winsome a Gabrielle, might make a tolerable king, — the Pavillon Marsan was sorely grieved, sorely displeased, at the undignified proceedings of the Élysée Bourbon. Serious dissensions were frequent in the family. The king declared that discord now troubled him more than his gout. But he had the wisdom to approve of the pursuits of the younger duchess, whose fondness for theatres, concerts, balls, and plays he thought only natural at her age, and far more commendable than the discussion of politics.

"It has been proved to me," he said, "that to the women and their politics I owe at least two-thirds of my adversaries! Madame la Duchesse de Berry does not meddle with politics; she has chosen the better part. Let her then continue to amuse herself."

Louis XVIII. was also a little disturbed at this time by two or three pretenders to the throne of France, each resting his claims on the asserted escape of Louis XVII. from the Temple. The first was Mathurin Bruneau, who was soon disposed of. A more troublesome, if not formidable, claimant was Henri Louis Hébert, *soi-disant* Baron de Richemont and Duc de Normandie.* Both in 1814 and 1815 he protested against the accession of Louis XVIII. Again in 1817 he gave the police some trouble, and much roused the ire of his sacred majesty, whose serenity being further disturbed by the contentions and opposite views of the different branches of the female part of his family, was moved to express himself very harshly.

From the king's commendation of the Duchesse de Berry from abstaining from politics, the friends and partisans of the banished Duc d'Orléans conceived the idea of using her influence to bring their chief back to Paris and his party.

The dowager Duchesse d'Orléans had frequently, but in vain, entreated the king not to prolong her son's banishment or to give heed to the calumnies of his enemies; she would herself be willing to be a guarantee for his loyalty. On the occasion of the marriage the duke had duly sent his congratulations, and expressed a

---

* This pretender went through a variety of adventures, always persisting in his claim, and defending his cause in memorials and pamphlets. He protested against Louis Philippe's elevation to the throne; was condemned to twelve years' imprisonment; escaped; and again and again was arrested. In 1848 he was allowed unmolested to pose as legitimate king; some old dowagers of the Faubourg St. Germain composed his court. He died in 1855.

desire to be allowed to offer his compliments in
person. Louis turned a deaf ear to this, but gave
him, and several others at that time, the grand
cross of the Legion of Honour. Again protesta-
tions of gratitude and eternal fidelity are received
from the illustrious exile, but they only raise a
cunning smile on the face of the *rusé* monarch.
"Let him stay where he is," he said; "he is a
man of honour, no doubt; but he has the misfortune to please my enemies. I am more at
ease when the sea lies between his virtue and
my distrust."

However, the Duchesse de Berry had more
than once expressed a wish to see her dear kind
aunt and uncle D'Orléans. Being urged by the
dowager duchess, she told the king that the presence of these dear relatives was alone wanting to
complete her happiness. He regretted to learn
that anything was wanting to make her happiness
perfect, and the more so that what was needed
was the very thing he could not grant. He
spoke to M. Decazes on the subject. He "verily
thought that public tranquillity would not be in
any way disturbed by the return of his serene
highness." This was clearly a gain to the
exile.

The king, however, thought it would be well to
discuss the matter with his fair friend the countess
at their next *tête-à-tête*. But she could not be
prevailed on to risk an opinion, for she knew that

the Duchesse d'Angoulême abhorred the Duc
d'Orléans, and was vehemently opposed to his
return. She was sure that "whatever his majesty might determine would be the wisest decision
that could be arrived at." This pleased the king.
He believed that she agreed with him, but forbore
to say so because the Comte d'Artois was of opinion that to recall the duke and load him with
favours was a surer way of securing his fidelity
and attachment to the interests of the elder
branch than banishing him from his country, on
the principle, probably, of heaping coals of fire
on one's adversary.

This opinion the count reiterated. "You treat
our cousin too severely," he said. "I am persuaded that his sentiments are in the main what
they ought to be." The little duchess in coaxing
terms once more said how she longed to see the
dear uncle who, when she was a child, had been so
kind to her.

Louis at last, against his better judgment,
yielded to the urgent entreaties of a part of his
family. The Duc d'Angoulême always adopted
the views of the duchess, and the Duc de
Berry was indifferent: "If Madame la Duchesse," he said, "would be made happier by
the return to France of the Duc d'Orléans, so
would he."

To the minister who presented the pen to the
king, for his signature to the order recalling the

Duc d'Orléans to France, he said, on returning it :
" Let this pen be kept; it will serve to sign the
abdication of those who urge me to commit this
fault " — prophetic words, indeed, if, as is asserted,
they really were uttered by Louis XVIII.

CHAPTER XXIII.

A Piece of Advice. — Enforcing His Claims. — Mother and Child Are Doing Well. — Assassinating the Duke. — Royal Visits, Balls and *Fêtes*. — Alexander's Parting Counsel. — The Duc de Berry Assassinated. — The Anteroom of the Opera-house.— The Closing Scene.

THE Duc d'Orléans and his family returned to France in February, 1817. He was received by the king with an appearance of cordiality while desiring not to see him at all. "*Mon cousin*," he said, "I shall hope to see you often at the château. Let your society be ours." This was meant, it appears, as a piece of advice, but was received by the duke as a compliment. He, however, did not act upon it, but immediately after his arrival began to busy himself with gathering together the remains of his paternal inheritance, and assembling around him his old clique.

Though he was most circumspect in his conduct, so that no reproach could be addressed to him, the Palais Royal was nevertheless regarded as the headquarters of intrigue and conspiracy; thus realising, as the king believed, his fears and expectations when he consented to his return. One obstacle to his views Louis resolved to oppose to him. This was an order that the princes of the royal house should not sit in the Chamber of Peers; by which means he prevented the Duc d'Orléans from speaking against any of the measures introduced by his ministry. He, however, was more intent at that time in seeking to add to his possessions.

Although he was immensely rich, his parsimony was the frequent subject of jests and epigrams; and the astonishment of the liberal party was great indeed when he brought an action against M. Julien to enforce the claim he made to the buildings comprising the Comédie Française. But he was less triumphant in this matter than he expected to be. The decision, as he ascertained, was almost certain to be against him. He therefore proposed a compromise, and to his immense chagrin had to hand over to M. Julien, the then proprietor of the building, the sum of 1,150,000 *francs* — between forty and fifty thousand pounds sterling.

It may perhaps have given him some sort of satisfaction, as the king, much mortified, believed it would, when on the 21st of September, 1819, the Duchesse de Berry gave birth to a daughter. Two previous premature confinements had disappointed the anxious hopes of the elder Bourbons. On the present occasion it was almost high treason to doubt the appearance of an heir; and the 101 guns were confidently listened for by all good royalists as the Virgin's reply to their earnest entreaties that a son might be vouchsafed to them. But neither prayers, nor votive offerings, nor revived street processions, had availed. Mother and child were doing well, and that must suffice for the present.

But, although the heir was not yet forthcoming, the throne that was supposed to await him was thought to be more satisfactorily established. France, released from the ignominious burden of the army of occupation, and the war indemnity paid, the nation might soon look to be herself again. Certainly Bonapartism, as it was called, had not been extirpated, severe as had been the repressive measures employed by the government. It was preserved in the army as a sort of religion, and excited in royalist circles considerable alarm as the time drew near for the final evacuation of France. A secret negotiation was attempted with a view of prolonging the stay of the foreign troops, and one means employed to create disquiet was a pretended attempt to assassinate the Duke of Wellington when returning at night from a reception at Lady Crawford's to his hôtel in the Rue de l'Élysée.

The duke's life was in no sort of danger. It was even asserted that he was concerned in the plot, therefore a party to the sham attack upon him. But this of course was an absurd story circulated by those who were not favourable to him, and they appear to have been numerous. Louis, however, or rather his Minister of Police, discovered this intrigue of "royalists more royalist than the king;" and the minister received his reward, *une superbe alliance*, as the king said — his royal master asking in marriage Mdlle. Sainte-Aulaire, a lady with an ample dowry and of an ancient royalist family, in order to bestow her hand on his minister as a particular mark of his favour.

But when the strong places of France began to be evacuated in November, 1818, according to the terms of the Convention agreed upon by the sovereigns at the Congress of Aix-la-Chapelle, the troops were escorted out of the towns by throngs of people, half frantic with joy at their departure, shouting " *Vive la France*," and singing with enthusiasm their patriotic songs. The Congress being dissolved, the Emperor Alexander, and his brother the Grand Duke Constantine, with the King of Prussia and his son, returned to Paris to take their final leave of the king. Court balls, grand banquets, *fêtes*, and public rejoicings were, as before, the order of the day. But the people were less sympathetic, for, notwithstanding all these gaieties, much financial embarrassment prevailed. There was a great depreciation in the public funds, and even a prospect of national bankruptcy.

At this crisis the Emperor Alexander came to

the rescue of France, and a prolongation of time for the payment of the indemnity was arranged. The czar is said to have then expressed his approval of Louis XVIII.'s political system. It was difficult to define exactly what that system was. Some writers have called it "playing the despot under the partial disguise of a constitutional king." At all events, he was then invited to become a party to the Holy Alliance, and he seems to have been rather elated in consequence, considering it a proof of the fear with which the foreign sovereigns regarded France from the moment they made her free.

The emperor warned the king as a parting counsel that he would do well to keep a vigilant eye on the proceedings of the Duc d'Orléans's friends. That the duke was ignorant of what was done and said in his name he sincerely hoped and desired to believe. "My cousin," replied the king, "is doubtless a man of honour, and would on no account plot against me; but if his friends could thrust me from my throne, and were to invite him to sit on it, he would not, I think, object to take my place, provided it appeared to him that he could sustain himself there."

By the 1st of July, 1819, the whole of the foreign troops had left. "God be praised!" exclaimed his sacred majesty. "At last I may believe that I am King of France. Gentlemen," he said, turning to the courtiers standing around

him, " henceforth I will be guarded only by my
own soldiers ; and I promise you, we shall be perfectly peaceful." The promise was not realised ;
yet, on the whole, it may be said that appearances
in 1819 — deceitful though they were — war-
ranted the hope of the Bourbons that the throne
for which an heir was so anxiously desired was at
last fairly established.

Lamentably, then, in 1820 were those hopes
suddenly dashed by the dagger of the assassin
Louvel, who, on the night of the 13th of February, stabbed the Duc de Berry as he was re-
entering the Opera-house, after conducting the
duchess to her carriage. " Adieu," he was saying
to his wife ; " I shall soon rejoin you " — for she
was leaving the theatre early, feeling nervous
from the effects of a blow she had received from
the sudden opening of a door in the corridor, as
she was passing out of the Duc d'Orléans's box
to her own. The man placed his hand on the
prince's shoulder, struck him under the right
breast, then fled with all speed up the Rue de
Richelieu. For the moment the prince thought it
only a blow ; but blood began to issue, and putting his hand to his side, he drew the dagger from
the wound. " *Voilà un fier brutal !* " he exclaimed,
and would have fallen but for the support of the
Comte de Menard, who stood near, but whom the
man Louvel had thrust aside to do his vile deed
more surely. All this took place so rapidly that

the duchess's carriage had not yet left.   Hearing
the duke's exclamation, she instantly jumped out,
opposing all attempts to restrain her, rushed to
her husband, and, while embracing him, her dress
was covered with his blood.

The prince was now removed to an anteroom
and laid on a sofa, and two surgeons were soon in
attendance.   Hope that he would survive there
was none.   He asked for a priest, and the Bishop
of Chartres shortly after arrived.   "Where is my
Caroline, my wife?" he cried.   "Oh! come to
me, that I may die in your arms."   She, meanwhile, was in an agony of grief, sobbing violently,
insisting on embracing him, her dress torn and
stained, her hair dishevelled, imploring the doctors
to speak to her words of hope.

Meanwhile the ballet was going on, and the
applause of the spectators was plainly heard;
what had taken place had not then been communicated to the manager.   Once the dying man
opened his eyes, and recognised the room he was
in.   "Ah, this room!" he exclaimed; "'tis a
judgment of heaven."   It was there that he had
been accustomed to have his rendezvous with the
figurantes of the Opéra.

The Princesse Adélaïde d'Orléans was so
deeply impressed by the horror of the scene in the
anteroom, and its incongruity with what was taking place outside, that, overcome by her feelings,
she fainted.

All of the family had assembled except the king, when the duke suddenly asked for his children, the baby princess, and the illegitimate family. Of the latter, the two girls only were brought to him ; but he whispered to his brother Angoulême, "The boy." No heed was given to this request ; perhaps it seemed too like a family acknowledgment of him. But, whether or not, the child was not brought to his father.

At last the king arrived. Life seemed to have been so long spared to the dying man that he might ask with his last breath that he who had given him his death-blow should not die for it. The king made no reply. He then asked pardon for disturbing him, for bringing him from his bed ; and Louis answered, "I have had my night's rest, my child. It is half-past five ; I shall not leave you again." Once more he said, imploringly, "Let him not die." Still no answer. He then asked to be turned on his left side, and, murmuring, "I should have died happier," breathed his last.

END OF THE FIRST VOLUME.

www.ingramcontent.com/pod-product-compliance
Lightning Source LLC
Chambersburg PA
CBHW021214090426
42740CB00006B/218